You
hold the power
to save lives — use it.

George Thomas

GOING THE DISTANCE

The George Thomas Story

George Thomas
&
Jeff Welsch

Sports Publishing L.L.C.
Champaign, Illinois

Photo Credits:
Page 88: Courtesy of Georgiann Rapp; Page 156: Courtesy of Richard Larsen
Page 159: Courtesy of Gary Brannan; All other photos courtesy of Norman C. Thomas.

Director of production: Susan M. Moyer
Project manager: Tracy Gaudreau
Developmental editor: Erin Linden-Levy
Copy editor: Cindy McNew
Dust jacket design: Joseph Brumleve

ISBN: 1-58261-629-9

Printed in the United States of America

Sports Publishing L.L.C.
www.sportspublishingllc.com

For Mom and Dad

— G. T.

For Sherry,
Who has taken me places I've never been

For Matt, Megan, and Jason

— J. W.

Contents

Acknowledgments

The authors wish to thank the following people for their advice, support and assistance in the completion of this project:

Norman and Edith Thomas, Edith Shelley, Sterling Thomas and Norman Thomas, for their tireless support; Terri Gooch, for her input, support and much, much more; Will Rotzler, for starting me in cycling; Hank Cunningham of Helotes Bicycle, for his friendship and mechanical skills; John Hughes, for his confidence in me; Steve Born, of E-Caps and Hammer Nutrition for his friendship, inspiration and wealth of nutritional knowledge; Muffy Ritz, for all of the fun rides and RAAM tips; Dwan Shepard of Co-Motion Cycles, for his friendship and unwavering support with bicycles and accessories; Katie Lindquist, my 2000 RAAM teammate; Rick Anderson, my 2000 RAAM crew chief; Meredith Thomas; Bev Thomas, for her recollections of RAAM 1995 and for her support through hard times both on and off the bike; Mike Kloeppel, for crewing all over the country, making ultra-racing fun and being the best crew person I've ever had—G.T.

Sherry Moore Welsch, the best editor I've ever had; Scott Stouder, a kindred spirit and the most selfless friend I've known; Jim Moore, for his insights and inspiration; Matt and Megan Welsch; Jason Moore-Greenke; Clifford Welsch and Kay Welsch; Martin and Dee Rotto; Ron Neumann and Susan Richardson—J.W.

Jerry Swille, whose belief in this project made it possible; Dr. Steven Schachter, who encouraged us to start this book; Jim Bunn; Gary Brannan, for his striking cover photo; Michael Shermer, whose book, *Race Across America: The Agonies & Glories of the World's Longest & Cruelest Race,* provided vivid RAAM descriptions and background—G.T. & J.W.

Foreword

At least once in a lifetime, you may be fortunate enough to meet someone truly inspirational, someone whose influence becomes a change agent in your life. I know this to be true, because I have met and been inspired by George Thomas.

As a neurologist who is privileged to care for people with epilepsy, my role is to help patients reach their potential in life. However, I did not appreciate what was really possible for my patients and indeed for any of us until I heard George talk and came to know him. His story is as much about the triumph of the human spirit as his incredible athletic achievements.

My admiration of George is shared by countless others who have met him and who will now read this book. He shares his most personal and painful experiences time and time again so that other people who are struggling with epilepsy may benefit. He stresses the importance of doctor-patient communication as one of the keys to healing. He sets big goals for himself. And he does it all with modesty and humility that belie his accomplishments.

George donated the bike frame that he rode cross-country on the Race Across America for an auction held by the Epilepsy Foundation of Massachusetts and Rhode Island. I am now its proud owner and often think of George and what he means to me and to people with epilepsy.

No matter where you are today on your journey, may this book inspire you to go the distance, to go beyond your epilepsy to your own greatness, and may you be reminded of your own possibilities every time you pick up this book and think of George.

—Steven C. Schachter, M.D.

Introduction

In the spring of 1998, George Thomas approached me with an idea I thought was just as zany as racing a bicycle across America in 10 days without any sleep.

Would I be interested, he asked, in telling the story of his life in a book?

I hemmed and I hawed. I knew from writing a feature story about him for the *Corvallis (Ore.) Gazette-Times* in 1995 that he had an interesting story to tell—an ordinary guy who had overcome a severe car accident and epilepsy to become an ultra-marathon bicycle racer.

But a book? I was skeptical.

After all, the only bicycle racer in the American public's sporting consciousness at the time was the incomparable Lance Armstrong, and this was before his book *It's Not About the Bike* was released. The only bicycle race of any national interest was the Tour de France; I had never even heard of the 3,000-mile Race Across America until I met George.

Moreover, like most of the smattering of people who knew just enough about RAAM, I figured he was a courageous man who must be a few spokes short of a full wheel.

I wondered: Who would publish such a book, much less buy it?

George didn't flinch at my apprehension. Instead he handed me a 30-minute video of his RAAM adventure in 1995 and asked me to take a look.

About a month later, I plugged in the video. About 20 minutes into the video, I called George. "Let's do a book," I said.

What I saw led me to believe that his story was bigger than any one individual, bigger than any one event, bigger even than any one debilitating disorder.

Sure, the images of George wilting in the 120-degree heat and careening to the pavement in a wee-hours driving rainstorm were riveting. And the descriptions of his rehabilitation from the car accident and dealing with subsequent violent seizures were gripping.

But what made the story so compelling was that George Thomas could've been Anyman.

He doesn't have the sky-walking athleticism of basketball star Kobe Bryant, the hand-eye coordination of baseball great Barry Bonds or the grace of hockey legend Wayne Gretzky. He couldn't have been a paid athlete in any of those sports even if he had spent every waking hour practicing.

In short, he's like the rest of us—an ordinary guy with an ordinary name who found the courage, discipline and intestinal fortitude to produce an extraordinary achievement.

I began to think there was a story here that could reach beyond the 2.1 million people worldwide who have epilepsy, the millions of Americans who bicycle and the thousands who are fascinated by extreme sports.

To seal the deal, George asked if I'd be interested in getting a taste of what ultra-marathon bicycle racing is all about. He invited me to join him for his inaugural Race Across Oregon, a 435-mile nonstop sprint from Ontario to Newport for the benefit of The Epilepsy Foundation of Oregon.

In June 1998, my wife, Sherry, and I followed as George alone battled a relay team of four ultra-fit cyclists and Oregon's fickle late-spring weather in what he described as a training ride.

The lingering memory of that event is of George rolling slowly into the artsy, faux-frontier community of Sisters just before midnight, stumbling off his bicycle and staggering with assistance into the back of his support van, where he lay nearly catatonic for 30 minutes.

Survive the race? I seriously wondered if he would survive at all.

When assured by friends Mike Kloeppel and Darren Snyder of his support crew that he would be okay, we moved ahead to the aptly named Tombstone Pass, high in Oregon's Cascade Range, where we fell asleep in the car and waited.

At 2:00 a.m., a surreal flashing of lights finally appeared from below, illuminating the thick stands of Douglas fir trees. The night's eerie silence was interrupted by the strains of the musical group R.E.M. playing over the van's mounted loudspeakers.

"I am, I am Superman ... and I know just what I am. I am, I am Superman ... and I can do anything."

Moments later, George arrived at the crest, tired but reinvigorated. The next time we saw him, at dawn, he pedaled past us in a blur and greeted us with a wide smile and a hearty, "Good morning! Isn't it a beautiful day?"

Superman, indeed.

Yes, I could see a story here.

Before I could fully understand George, who he was and why he chose to ride solo in the 1995 RAAM—before I could truly capture his essence in a book—we both agreed that the project would be best served if I witnessed firsthand the extraordinary event that is the Race Across America.

In the summer of 2000, Sherry and I joined his crew for the 2,975-mile odyssey from Portland, Oregon to Pensacola, Florida in which he was riding a tandem bicycle with Katie Lindquist of Plymouth, Minnesota.

As I researched the event, I came across staggering numbers—not the least of which was that exercise physiologists rate RAAM the most arduous sporting event in the world, well ahead of the Hawaii Ironman Triathlon, the Iditarod sled-dog race, and yes, the Tour de France.

George and Katie would burn 8,000-10,000 calories per day. They would pedal for an average of 21 hours. They would likely face nearly every type of weather imaginable—from blistering heat to freezing cold, from gale-force headwinds to pounding rains, and from the thin air of 10,000-foot altitudes to the suffocating humidity of the Deep South.

Most of all, they would face the merciless sleep deprivation and hallucinations for which RAAM is so notorious.

For 12 unforgettable days, we crossed the country at 13 mph, traversing back roads that provided us snapshots of a dying Americana that's being gobbled up an acre at a time by chain stores, restaurants and the electronic age.

As crew members, we had to remain focused for the entire journey, ensuring that George and Katie would remain safe, receive enough nutrition and have their every need met. We would secure motels for their three hours of sleep, find 24-hour grocery stores to resupply the mountains of ice, search for laundromats and try to break up the monotony of the road by reading supportive e-mails from back home over the loudspeakers atop the van.

When it was over, and the crew could all let down its guard for the first time in two weeks, many wept.

In 23 years as a sports writer, I've covered many memorable events and people—NCAA championships, professional sports, Heisman Trophy winners and Hall of Fame coaches—but never have I witnessed an event quite like RAAM.

There was, I was more confident than ever, a story here.

Any lingering doubts I had about public interest in a book about an ordinary guy achieving extraordinary feats were erased upon our return to Corvallis.

I had decided to chronicle the event for the *Gazette-Times*, thinking RAAM might offer our diverse community a welcome break from the endless litany of seasonal ball sports.

The response was stunning, unlike any I've ever witnessed over a sports story in my 12 years at the paper.

For months, I was approached on the streets nearly every day by readers—acquaintances and strangers alike—who were riveted by George and Katie's excellent adventure.

One couple told me they raced each other to the door every morning to get the next installment in the daily paper. The winner got the sports section; the loser had to make coffee.

There was definitely a book here.

It was clear that George Thomas's story struck an inspirational chord with the average person.

Count me among them. Before knowing George, the longest I'd ever ridden a bicycle was 50 miles. This past summer, I just finished my fourth Race Across Oregon as a member of a relay team, a feat unthinkable a mere five years ago.

Therein lies the heart of the story.

To paraphrase Lance Armstrong, it really isn't about the bike.

It's about life.

It's about meeting challenges head on without blinking. It's about problem solving in the face of every imaginable obstacle. It's about hours of monotony punctuated by fits of exhilaration.

It's about pain and suffering and it's about pride and ecstasy.

Above all, it's about *Going the Distance.*

—Jeff Welsch
September 2002

July 27, 1995
Palm Springs, California

Twenty-one solo cyclists begin the Race Across America in oppressive 125-degree heat, which forces several out of the race in the Mojave Desert, less than 150 miles from the start in Irvine, California ... Veterans Rob Kish and Danny Chew are the favorites but figure to be challenged by powerful women Seana Hogan and Muffy Ritz ... Steve Born drops out because of viral problems ... George Thomas is in the middle of the pack as the riders cross the San Gabriel Mountains.

Chapter One

July 27, 1995

I hate throwing up.

I *really* hate throwing up. Nobody likes it, of course, but for me it's especially unpleasant. It elicits memories of an episode that was both life-altering and terrifying. Throwing up once is once too many for me. Twice crosses the line.

> *Oh no, not again ... this morning was bad enough ... but at least then it was at the Holiday Inn ...*

I had been preparing for this day—the first day of the 2,911-mile bicycle Race Across America (RAAM)—for more than a decade in one way or another. This obscure and incomparably challenging sporting event, and all that it had come to mean, had already exacted a climactic toll on my frayed nerves on that first morning. I was hoping to exude confidence when I rolled to the starting line in Irvine, California, but instead I found myself gagging in a bathroom at the race's hotel headquarters.

Solo racers line up in Irvine, California to start the 1995 RAAM.

Now, after pedaling the trepidation out of my system for more than six hours from the coast and through the San Gabriel Mountains, I was riding unevenly into the suffocating blast furnace called the Mojave Desert. I was barely 120 miles into RAAM and I was beginning to feel that queasy inevitability in my stomach again.

A fellow endurance cyclist once described racing in hot, dry weather as akin to pedaling into a blow dryer— the opposite of wind chill. It is an apt analogy. The thermometer just outside of Palm Springs read 126. On the shimmering asphalt of the Interstate 10 frontage road it was over 140. I was in nature's oven.

... this is unreal ... can I take this? ... no relief, no shade, no cooling breeze ... careful where you put your hands, the brake levers will burn your fingers ... my eyes are burning ... water isn't helping ... it dries too fast! ... ice doesn't help, either; it melts too fast ... I'd give anything to cool off ... no, I just want to get OUT of here ... the only way to do that is to keep pedaling ... don't know if I can ...

My mouth was so dry I struggled to talk to my support crew as they pulled alongside me in their air-conditioned blue Windstar minivan to check on my condition. The bread they were feeding me through the window as we rolled along at 18 mph instantly went dry. I had no saliva, so the only way to eat was to moisten the bread. We decided the easiest way to moisten the bread was to use mayonnaise. I hate mayonnaise, but I had little choice. I had to keep eating to replenish the calories I was burning. The crew used so much mayo that it squirted all over my hands and fingerless cycling gloves. When I wiped it off on my shorts the black lycra literally burned my hands.

Relief came in the form of a water backpack, called a CamelBak, filled with ice, but it was temporary. Within minutes, the ice melted. The water in the uninsulated tube leading from the pack was so hot that unless I remembered to empty it manually the first swig would burn my throat.

I tried to amuse myself by yearning for the cold, wet, snowy rides I'd shivered through while training in the lush mountains near my home in the Willamette Valley of western Oregon. I'd always wished for heat. Now the old cliché popped into my head: "Be careful what you wish for."

... this is unbearable ... I want to stop so badly ... got to get out of here ... where to find relief? In the air-conditioned van? Or by getting to Arizona? ... tough choice ... not really ... Gotta get to Arizona ...

Incredibly, I had felt strong and fresh as I pedaled over the San Gabriels on the first leg of this nonstop journey to Savannah, Georgia. It was merely a desert mirage. I was learning the first of many harsh RAAM lessons.

Exercise physiologists describe RAAM as the most arduous sporting event in the world—more difficult than the Iditarod sled-dog race, Hawaii's Ironman Triathlon and the more visible Tour de France bicycle race. To the casual observer, the Race Across America is an exercise in masochism at best and insanity at worst. What separates RAAM from the world's other grueling events isn't the extraordinary exertion of energy; it's the sleep deprivation and psychological strain.

The Tour de France has a deserved reputation as one of the toughest events in any sport. Cyclists pedal all-out for several hours against each other and the elements, retire to motel rooms for food and rest, and then repeat the cycle every day for three weeks. RAAM pits riders against the same natural challenges—heat, mountain climbs, twisting descents, headwinds, cold and rain, and then adds hours of tedium and sleeplessness. We pedal day and night, trying to cover 300-350 miles daily as quickly as possible. We rest anywhere from one to four hours. Our bodies become energy-consuming machines, burning 8,000-10,000 calories daily, the equivalent of about 40 large cinnamon rolls or 30 cheeseburgers.

... gotta eat ... don't want to eat ... no more mayonnaise, please! ... a Slim Fast or a Boost, maybe? ... don't know if I can stomach them ... they get so hot so fast ... crackers? ... no, too hard to chew and even harder to swallow ... it's SOOOO hot ... if you don't eat, you won't make it ... but what to eat? ... what to drink? ... This is getting scary ...

For all the physical challenges, the most ominous obstacles in RAAM are emotional. The endless hours of exertion and lack of sleep conspire to turn cyclists into pedaling zombies. Hallucinations from sleep deprivation are legend among ultra-cyclists. Stories range from my own vision of a 60-foot-tall pizza delivery boy rising from the swamp at 3 a.m. to minivans turning into Minnie Mouse and preachers pedaling alongside a cyclist at 20 mph through the night. Once a RAAM competitor rode 2,500 miles, stopped abruptly at a bridge and refused to continue, insisting to his crew that aliens were lurking underneath. The only solution was a nap. After four hours of sleep, he sheepishly crossed the bridge and continued to the finish.

The only cure for fatigue is rest, but there is little time for sleep until RAAM ends after eight to twelve days of riding. Every minute you're off the bike you know that the leaders are riding away, increasing the gap with every stroke. Adding to the rider's list of nightmares is the fear of falling so far behind that he or she not only has no chance to win, but also risks arriving more than 48 hours behind the leader and failing to earn a RAAM ring as an official finisher. And that's the only prize in RAAM. The race truly is all about reaching for the ring, because there are no other tangible rewards. No money, no glory, no hype. Many finish the race alone, in the middle of the night, greeted only by a handful of race officials, the crew and perhaps a spouse.

> *... sleep deprivation? ... I hope that's something I eventually have to face ... the race is only six hours old and I'm barely moving ... this is so embarrassing ... quit thinking like that! ... come on, come on, keep moving ... ride until dark, then it'll cool off and you can pick up your speed ... but will it cool off? ... it has to ... it HAS to ... don't know how much longer I can take this heat ...*

This much I knew: I had to stay on the bicycle. It's a cardinal rule of endurance racing. Dismounting costs precious minutes, even during a 3,000-mile race. It can also create an impenetrable barrier in an already-fragile psyche. Getting off the bicycle might mean never getting back on. For these reasons, ultra-cyclists learn to eat, drink and change clothes on the bicycle. Some even urinate from the saddle in a remarkable display of balance, coordination and aim.

Why did I choose such a brutal, thankless, unforgiving event in which to prove my mettle? The reasons would be obvious to any armchair psychologist.

Twice in the previous decade I had spiraled to the proverbial bottom, physically and emotionally. In 1984, an alleged drunken driver plowed into me while I was standing in a friend's front yard in my native San Antonio, Texas, nearly killing me, mangling my body and leaving me forever with a neurological disorder called epilepsy. In 1989, after five years of mysterious but otherwise unremarkable minor dizzy spells, I suffered my first severe seizure while on a trip taken shortly after my honeymoon. For the next five months the seizures were so violent that

I once nearly drowned in my own vomit. The effects of medications, none of which controlled the seizures, were so debilitating that I became a virtual invalid.

I began to wonder if I would spend the rest of my life in bed until a then experimental drug finally reined in the seizures. But the experiences had sapped every last ounce of my self-worth. I lost my job, my driver's license and my dignity. I viewed myself as abnormal. In seeking balance, my emotional pendulum swung wildly to the opposite extreme. I chose one of the most difficult human endeavors possible, one that would challenge every fiber of my being, yet was consistent with a lifelong interest and the source of my major successes.

I chose the Race Across America.

As outlandish as the notion might seem, if I was to insist upon an extreme sporting event for my self-imposed therapy, then RAAM was a natural. Although I enjoyed the traditional ball sports on a recreational level growing up, I lacked the coordination and quickness required for higher performance. As a runner, I didn't have much speed, so success came mostly in cross-country, where longer distances were more to my liking. The same applied to bicycle racing. While I did okay at shorter distances, I found that I actually had some talent for longer events.

Though I dreamed of being a finely tuned athlete like Greg LeMond in the Tour de France or Alexi Grewal in the 1984 Olympic road race, I realized my limitations. Long distance events are more about sheer will and pain tolerance than hand-eye coordination or foot skills. RAAM captivated me like no other sport when I read about it in a cycling magazine in 1982. Then I was riveted to it on ABC's *Wide World of Sports* in 1983, a year after it began with four riders as the Great American Bike Race. I admired those four soloists. They struck me as incredibly tough, resilient and courageous.

In essence, I had been preparing for my 1995 RAAM journey for 13 years. For the first few years, it was simply a dream harbored by an unmotivated college student who loved to race his bike but wasn't thrilled with training. After my accident in 1984, it was a lofty goal for a blossoming radio personality who finally had some direction. In the wake of my seizures in 1989, it became a mission.

> *... what am I doing out here? ... everyone looks so fit and I've only trained for six weeks! ... there are a million things I'd rather be doing ... I feel fried ... it's so hot ... six hours? That's all I've been out here? ... what is my crew thinking? ... you're such a wimp ... I'm trying, but ... am I in last place? ... where is everyone else? ... are they as hot as I am? ... I'm not ready for this heat ... oh, here comes my crew ... they look so happy! ... are they having fun? ... maybe I'm doing all right ... other than the heat, I feel strong ... what is Bruce trying to give me? ... vitamins? ... you've got to be kidding me ... just thinking about vitamins is making me gag ... oh well ... oh no ... now I'm in real trouble ...*

After pedaling along at a steady and comfortable 18-20 mph since the start, suddenly I was wobbling below 10. My skin burned bright red. I was sticky with sunscreen, dried sweat and spilled energy drink. The vitamins were making me nauseous. Despite the heat, my teeth began to chatter and I felt chills—the early symptoms of heat stroke. At that point, I had one thought.

Stop.

As I veered my Serotta titanium bicycle off the frontage road, I felt like I was pedaling in mud. I looked down and saw that my thin racing tires were carving small grooves in the mushy asphalt. Clumsily, I lifted my leg over the top tube of my bicycle and staggered on my cleats to the pace van where my friend from Oregon, Mike Kloeppel, was waiting to help me into the air-conditioning. I rewarded his kindness by vomiting again, all over his shoes.

The only smiles were on the faces of an accompanying camera crew hired by my primary sponsor, a pharmaceutical company called GlaxoSmithKline. They were looking for high drama and were already blessed with more than they could have scripted. Race cofounder Michael Shermer once described RAAM as "long periods of boredom punctuated by short bursts of terror." The film crew was reveling in my terror.

Here I was, on the eastern outskirts of Palm Springs, well before RAAM's notorious mountain passes, Plains winds and sleep deprivation had any chance to exact a price, and already I was losing it both physically and mentally, fading in the heat and foolishly wasting energy with embarrassment. Within minutes of feeling relatively strong, I had disintegrated to a state where simply summoning the willpower to leave the comforts of the van would be an accomplishment.

> *... sponge bath with ice water ... so cold, but still so hot ... can't believe I'm shivering ... sorry about your shoes, Mike ... what are you doing? ... why are you making me get up? ... I don't want to leave the air-conditioning ... I know I was supposed to get to Prescott before stopping ... I know I've got to keep moving ...*

George spends a few moments with friend and competitor
Steve Born at the start of solo RAAM in 1995.

*don't want to ... got to move ... that stop sign
at the end of the road looks like a good place for
another break ... no ... it feels so good in here
... MOVE! ...*

Lesson learned: I had envisioned this journey to be fun. It wasn't. I had dreamed of an adventure. It wasn't. I was in a race—a long, difficult race, in part against 18 other men and three women, all better prepared than I, but even more against the elements and the unique demons that haunt RAAM.

Nobody in my crew would've blamed me if I had quit right there on the scorched earth. After all, I was an ordinary guy who was attempting an extraordinary feat. Though I had twice completed RAAM as a member of a four-man relay team from San Antonio, I had no clue about the task I was undertaking as a soloist. I had precious little serious training. My longest race had been 510 miles. I was taking medication for epilepsy. It hadn't been too many years earlier that simply pedaling around the block was a monumental achievement. I was a dreamer. My fanciful dreams had placed me in this brutal reality. It would take more than wishful thinking to get me out.

*... you're going to make it ... you HAVE to
make it ... this is why you're here ... this is what
it's all about ... quitting is not an option ...*

I gathered my thoughts and decided that the only way I could keep my promise to myself was to approach the rest of RAAM the way I was forced to approach life while recovering from the accident and seizures: One hour, one pedal stroke, one breath at a time. If I focused on the big picture, it was too daunting. I readjusted my game plan in my head. I would set small goals, accomplish them, and then move on to the next. Instead of a 3,000-mile race, RAAM would become a series of 300 ten-mile races. Or 600 five-mile races. Whatever it took.

The only unacceptable option was quitting.

I stirred in the van, choked down some water and reluctantly summoned the strength to stumble back into the oppressive heat. I climbed on my bicycle and headed east toward the Colorado River. Within 10 miles, I stopped and returned to the van for more water. It wasn't as if I was going to quit; it was simply that I had to stop to keep going.

160 miles into the race, just before dusk, I began the climb from 500 feet below sea level to 1,900-foot Chiriaco Summit. I felt strong and was excited that nightfall was approaching. But less than a mile from the top, in 115-degree heat, I again felt the familiar chills of heat stroke. My crew used cups and squirt guns to douse me with water. At the top, I dismounted again and returned to the van. I noticed other riders on the side of the road, including one who was taking a shower behind a makeshift curtain. I was shivering and disoriented. My crotch was raw from the soaking my shorts and chamois pad were getting from my well-meaning crew.

Unbeknownst to me, my good friend Steve Born of Ketchum, Idaho, had already surrendered to the heat and dropped out. So had several others. My crew kept this information from me for fear that I would become distracted by Born's fate. I returned to my bicycle and headed down the pass in the darkness. Less than an hour later, I found myself in the coolness of the pace van one more time. It was nearing 2 a.m. One after another, riders who had stopped during the worst of the heat passed me.

... riders are passing ... maybe I haven't been riding so badly after all ... it's dark ... why hasn't it cooled off? ... You ride well at night ... you should be moving right now ... you're losing more time ... maybe I'm not so weak after all ... gotta keep moving ... I'm sick of stopping, but I keep getting sick ... we have to fix this, and fix this now ...

Crew chief Bruce Franklin, who was overseeing the three-person day crew, had been giving me a steady diet of water and energy drinks to keep me hydrated, but now he was driving toward Blythe, California, in the second support van to find a motel and catch a nap. My wife, Bev, who was in charge of the three-person night crew, had been arguing for much of the afternoon for an IV with saline solution. My inclination was to side with Bruce. I only knew a catheter as a tube inserted into a private part of the male anatomy. And due to an oversight on my part, perhaps subconsciously intentional, we only had one IV catheter, which meant it was a one-shot deal. Once I had the IV, we wouldn't be able to give me another one once it was removed. Trouble was, at 5 a.m. it was already over 100 degrees. I was okay now, but what about mid-afternoon when temperatures likely would hit 120 again in the Arizona desert?

With Bruce temporarily out of the picture, Bev prevailed. Amid the mounds of supplies was but one catheter, donated from my brother Sterling's veterinary clinic in Oregon. Team medic Sabra Thomas inserted the tiny needle in my arm and squeezed the saline bag. It barely dripped. Was there blockage? Sabra quickly realized the catheter was gauged for cats and began squeezing the drip bag as hard as possible to force quicker movement. It worked! Though I wasn't aware of it, the heat and debate over my treatment had conspired to create a power struggle that would drive a wedge between the two crews, especially between Bev and Bruce, as the days passed. But all that mattered to me now was that the IV worked. I was relieved beyond description and instantly rejuvenated.

In the soothing silence of the wee hours, I boarded my Serotta again and pedaled in the headlights of the pace van driven by Bev. My parents, Norm and Edith Thomas, and my aunt, Georgiann Rapp, were long gone, having driven their Road Trek motor home ahead with the day crew. They needed sleep to prepare for a second day now shrouded in uncertainty.

I was alone with my thoughts, my bike and a rubber band I wrapped around my wrist to snap if I felt myself drifting off to sleep or having a hallucination. As I rode on the shoulder of I-10 into Blythe, a small town hard on the banks of the Colorado River at the Arizona border, the sun was just beginning to peek over the barren Kofa Mountains to the east. The opening day of RAAM had been an unbelievable roller-coaster ride, the first of many that would push me to physical and emotional brinks.

I was back in basic survival mode, just like in the days after the accident and seizures. One breath, one pedal stroke, one hour at a time. I knew that pain, fatigue and the fear of failing to earn a ring would be my constant companions for the duration. I realized that the agonies of Day 1 were only a taste of what lay ahead. I was 150 miles behind schedule. I had lost 10 hours off the bike. The 48-hour cutoff window already was a worry. The nine-day plan was obsolete. I was tired and embarrassed, but also driven by newfound resolve.

... unless bones are poking through my
skin, I WILL finish this race ...

Now, as in 1984 and 1989, quitting simply was not an option.

July 28, 1995
Flagstaff, Arizona

As the cyclists leave the 118-degree temperatures of the desert, they climb through the mountains of Arizona, with Rob Kish, Danny Chew, Seana Hogan, Muffy Ritz, Tom Davies and Bruno Heer leading the way ... In the second tier of cyclists are rookies Dieter Weik, Beat Gfeller, Kaname Sakurai, Reed Finfrock and George Thomas, along with Rickey Wray Wilson, Gerry Tatrai and Terry Wilson.

Chapter Two

July 28, 1995

I was at once frustrated and motivated as I rode out of Blythe, California, just after dawn on the second day of the Race Across America. I had been excited about riding at night, yet I was only 200 miles into the race. Our plan had called for reaching the mountain town of Prescott, Arizona, more than 350 miles from the start.

> *... hmmmm ... a new day ... not especially happy to see you, sun ...*

The approaching dawn changed my surroundings to a beautiful rose color. The vivid landscapes buoyed my spirits. Still, I wasn't proud of my efforts. I had survived the first day, but I hadn't thrived. That wasn't good enough. After all, I had a hierarchy of goals for Race Across America. Most important, I wanted to finish officially, to complete the course within 48 hours of the winner. I wanted to maintain my friendships with my crew. I wanted to finish in less than 10 days. I wanted to be Rookie of the Year.

And I wanted to win.

An official finish might seem a routine goal, but in RAAM it's a feat unto itself. Typically half the cyclists quit. While I could drop out and still keep my friendships, the other goals were moot without an official finish.

Maintaining friendships among the crew is no small feat either. My crew consisted of nine friends and family members who were split into three groups driving three separate vehicles. The day crew consisted of chief Bruce Franklin, mechanic Michael Kloeppel and massage therapist Rena Andrews, all from my adopted home state of Oregon. The night crew was my wife and co-crew chief Bev, mechanic Eric Larsen of Cedarburg, Wisconsin, and certified emergency technician Sabra Thomas, my brother Sterling's former wife. My parents, Norman and Edith Thomas of San Antonio, along with my aunt, Georgiann, drove their motor home for backup.

They would be together in three separate, frequently bisecting groups almost constantly, confined to seamy vans and cramped motel rooms. For me to have a successful crossing, these people had to coexist in those extremely close quarters with lousy food, infrequent showers and precious little sleep. They had to remain alert for driving, navigating, mixing energy drinks, preparing food, doing laundry and much more while cruising at the snail's pace of 15 mph, usually in stifling heat. They had to maintain a cheerful mood around a cyclist who was never riding fast enough, was often cranky and needed continuous attention. Their paths would cross only periodically, usually for crew changes, but they were always on the ubiquitous walkie-talkies, discussing and sometimes arguing about how to best take care of me.

Adding to the mix was the four-person camera crew hired by GlaxoSmithKline. They were ordered to be thorough, so I often had a camera in my face at inopportune times—in the shower, when I relieved myself by the road or simply trying to find the will to push forward on my bicycle. I enjoyed their company, but there were times when they felt intrusive. Some in the crew felt the same way. It didn't help that the camera crew seemed cynical about this obscure event and me.

The exhaustion, heat and unrelenting stress were a 10-day recipe for frayed nerves and occasional road rage. The potential for conflict was enormous.

Our prerace strategy was simple. The day and night crews would alternate 12-hour shifts, starting at the race's beginning at noon Eastern Standard Time on July 27, 1995 (it was 9 a.m. at the actual start in Irvine, Calif., but because the finish was on the East Coast, race time was always recorded in EST).

When the night crew was off duty, they were to drive ahead, get a motel and rest. Our daily mileage goal was 300, meaning the night crew was to drive approximately 150 miles ahead to search for a motel. Twelve hours on and off sounded practical, but after subtracting time for driving ahead, locating and checking into a motel, showering, eating, waking, cleaning the van, laundry, etc., they were left with less than five hours to sleep—and that was if all went as planned. Crew changes ideally would occur at the motel, where the day crew could then take its break. When they woke, they would drive until they caught us.

The strategy lasted less than a day. My painstaking pace through the desert confused the crew. They didn't know what to do. Tension between the day and night crews flared before we got out of California.

The debate over use of the catheter was a prime example. It unnerved me to have the two crews barking at each other. I lost focus, which was the worst possible outcome. I quickly learned that I had to ignore their arguments.

When the catheter was finally inserted at Bev's insistence over Bruce's objections, it did provide an amazing change. My improved condition carried me into the Arizona sauna with high spirits and a steady pace. My fear of the heat dissipated.

Still, there was the question of what to do with the catheter once it had performed its duties. Once a catheter is removed, it is useless. Yet several days of desert riding lay ahead, so it was likely I'd need one again to mitigate the effects of the heat. Simply riding with the catheter in my arm was the other option, but that left the very real fear of infection. RAAM is not a clean sport. The support cars carry three sweaty, grungy crew members along with open food, soiled eating utensils, water, ice chests and everyone's clothes—some clean and some dirty. Meanwhile, the rider is on the road at least 21 shower-free hours per day, reeking of sweat, covered in dust and sticky with spilled food and old sunscreen.

My crew fretted about what to do with our lone needle. They didn't know.

"Just leave it taped in my arm," I finally said.

> *... can't believe how fresh I feel ... it's hot,*
> *but I can take this ... where is everybody else?*

The confidence gained from the knowledge that we could use another IV if necessary increased my speed. I went from survival mode to racing mode. I wanted to start catching people.

"What place am I in?" I asked my crew.

"Sixth," they reported.

> *... sixth? ... are you kidding me? ... feels*
> *like I'm 13ᵗʰ or 14ᵗʰ ... no way—I stopped too*
> *often last night ... too many riders passed me*
> *... if I'm in sixth, who's ahead of me? ... who's*
> *behind me?*

I asked for names. My crew couldn't produce any, but they were convincing. I rode on, thinking I was sixth.

Moments later, race director and cofounder Michael Shermer pulled alongside in an official race vehicle and we began to chat.

"Gee, what is it—only 115 today?" I joked, thinking the temperature was down to a cool 90 degrees or so.

"It's 118," Shermer replied.

I gulped. It felt so much cooler than the previous day's 126.

"How are you doing?" Shermer continued.

"I can't believe I'm in sixth place," I replied.

"You're not."

My heart sank. Shermer had reaffirmed my suspicions. I was 13ᵗʰ. Worse was the realization that my crew had let me down. I had put my complete trust in these people and they had either lied or were using mind games to keep me motivated. Either way, it was disappointing and discouraging. How could I trust them over the next 2,700 miles? I simmered for a few miles and avoided contact with them. I reminded myself that they had given up three weeks of their summer for no pay and little glory, but a sense of frustration took hold.

I forged ahead, feeling strong but alone.

After Shermer left, I started passing riders as we veered off Interstate 10 to the northeast on U.S. Highway 60 toward Wickenburg, Arizona. First it was Kaname Sakurai, a 30-year-old rookie from Nagoya, Japan. Then fellow rookie Dieter Weik, a 32-year-old German transplant who lived in Ridgecrest, California. Next came Rickey Wray Wilson, 41, of Arlington, Texas. We started our first major climb, the Yarnell grade, which rises 2,000 feet in less than 10 miles. I was surprised at my power.

My crew, which had been dumping water on me the previous day, was running alongside me excitedly. They played leapfrog with me in their vans, stopping to take pictures at strategic locations. They felt the same surge of adrenaline.

I was more in my element now. Temperatures had dipped. I began to notice juniper, then ponderosa pines as the elevation increased. It reminded me of the east side of the Cascade Mountains of Oregon, my home state. I was back on my liquid diet. The crew and I were back in sync.

Race director Michael Shermer keeps pace with George and tells him that he is 13th, not sixth.

Passing people made me feel competitive. At the summit of another twisting climb, just past Wickenburg, I went around another rider, Terry Wilson of Indianapolis. By the time I reached our first scheduled sleep stop in Prescott, it had cooled to the point where I needed to add clothes. I was energetic, awake and eager to continue.

This was the RAAM I had envisioned.

A motel room was set up with a massage table and food, but I had no desire to stop. Conditions had changed. I felt so fresh. The weather was perfect. In the back of my mind, I rehashed my desert miseries and pondered the perils ahead. I wanted to ride away from the memories as quickly as possible and exploit my newfound strength.

> *… gotta keeping moving … you know this isn't going to last … you may have conquered this, but you know you're not done …*

I trusted my judgment, but I also knew that the crew chief must be given almost complete authority on RAAM. The cyclist's job is to ride and provide updates on physical and emotional issues. The rest must be left to the crew, and that includes finding places for sleep breaks, food and a shower. They knew there were no motels between Prescott and Flagstaff. Bruce did not want me sleeping in the van in my dirty, sweaty, smelly clothes.

I finally talked myself into it by thinking about a snooze on the massage table. It sounded blissful. So I relented.

I climbed into the bathtub, followed by the camera crew, headed to the massage table, where I fell asleep, and then went to the bed, stretching out with eyes wide open. Rena moved me back to the massage table, where I drifted off again under the rhythmic motions of her hands. But I had been awake far too long, and when I did rise from a two-hour nap I didn't feel refreshed. Outside, in the 5,000-foot altitude of Prescott, there was a chill in the air, so I donned a jacket and tights. It felt so strange to shiver from cold instead of heat prostration.

I moved from Highway 89 onto Interstate 40 in northern Arizona and learned at Time Station 8 in the small town of Williams that Dieter Weik had passed me while I was sleeping. I woke up thinking I was still ahead of him, so I wasn't happy about this development. But it did give me a focus. I never truly expected to win, but I did want to be top rookie. I was buoyant again as I pedaled with purpose into the darkness to Flagstaff.

That's when my RAAM roller coaster suddenly began to take another plunge.

It started with little twinges in my Achilles tendon, an ache I hadn't previously experienced. After a few hours, the pain worsened, and when I'd try to rise out of the saddle for strength on climbs, I couldn't. My spirits had risen with the elevation, but now at 7,000 feet my bubble was bursting.

Another serious obstacle was in my path. I summoned my crew and we talked about solutions.

I had three words for them: Just fix it.

They were the same three words I'd uttered to my neurologist six years earlier.

———————

In 1989, I was living my dream. Ever since seventh grade, when my family took the first of what would become annual ski trips to Crested Butte, Colorado, I'd wanted to be a ski instructor.

I had quit graduate school at Stephen F. Austin State University in Nacogdoches, Texas, in 1987 to teach skiing full-time. I landed a job at Hoodoo Ski Bowl, a small resort in the Cascade Mountains of Oregon, then moved to nearby Mount Bachelor, a major ski resort near Bend. I skied all day, every day. When I wasn't teaching, I worked with the school's technical directors to improve my instructor skills. Five years after the car accident in San Antonio, my life was finally coming together. I was achieving my goals and living in one of the most beautiful areas of the country. I'd found my niche—a life I was passionate about, a life I wanted for a career.

For the first time, I was learning the meaning of commitment.

I was committed to something: My job. And I was committed to someone: An active and personable native Oregonian named Bevely Lewis.

Bev and I met on a rock-climbing blind date set up by Sterling, Sabra and a few friends. We hit it off immediately and soon were engaged. We married in March 1989 in a Presbyterian church in Bev's hometown of Corvallis, Oregon, and honeymooned on the island of Maui.

My happiness and good fortune obscured a nagging health issue that I largely ignored.

Ever since the car accident in 1984, I had experienced occasional dizzy spells that left me disoriented and nauseated. At first they were relatively infrequent, and I was so focused on rehabilitating my legs that I ignored the lightheadedness.

Over time, the frequency and intensity increased. I worried, but a visit to the doctor revealed little more than an iron deficiency. It was nothing that an improved diet wouldn't resolve. Though skeptical, I accepted the diagnosis. If something was really wrong, I didn't want to know.

A diet change had no effect. The dizzy spells continued. I'd have them skiing, on the chairlift, in the car. They came without warning. They affected my balance and left me weak and nauseated. I worried that my skiing would suffer. One day I was so dizzy I leaned against the lockers in the staff room at Mount Bachelor, wondering what would happen if I were on a chairlift. I was so weak I had to rest. I skipped teaching and took the day off.

It was then that Bev began to mention the "E" word. Epilepsy. I dismissed it as an overreaction. Life was good. I was happy. I didn't want or need the negativity. I ignored the warning signals and wished them away.

More important matters were at hand. I was at a crossroads. I dreamt of a life and career on the slopes, working at ski areas in the winter and at racing camps in the summer. If I could pass a rigorous certification exam, my income would increase and job opportunities would beckon. We could stay in the Pacific Northwest. It wouldn't be easy; the exam had a 33 percent pass rate. I focused all my energies and concentration on a test that would chart my future.

I aced it on my first try.

Soon after, when skiing season ended in May, Bev and I drove to San Antonio for a reception with friends who couldn't attend our wedding in Oregon. We took our four-wheel-drive Subaru station wagon. On the return trip, we began having problems with a troublesome rear axle just outside of Flagstaff, Arizona, so we stopped, left the car at the car dealership, checked into a room at the Motel 6, secured a car from Rent-A-Wreck and drove to the Grand Canyon.

I had a minor dizzy spell while driving to the canyon, but I shrugged it off. I didn't even tell Bev.

The next morning, I awoke and headed for the shower. The dizziness returned, only this spell was frighteningly powerful. The next thing I knew I was lying naked on the floor of the motel bathroom with an aching head. I could see Bev's worried face, spinning like a kaleidoscope.

The spinning soon stopped and I thought I'd be okay. Though Bev was worried, we didn't call an ambulance or go to the hospital. I thought it was an aberration. We went to a movie that night and avoided any talk about my episode.

The following morning, I was standing at the bathroom sink at the same motel, preparing to brush my teeth, when it came again, only even more profound than the previous day. I was so disoriented that I began to brush my reflection in the mirror.

As I stood looking at my spinning image in the mirror, I finally had to admit it to myself: Something was seriously wrong.

I staggered out of the bathroom and collapsed on the carpet at Bev's feet. Through my range of emotions I wondered what she was thinking about the man she had decided to marry. I wasn't even sure what to think of myself. For the first time, I felt helpless. It was a feeling I would know well in the coming months.

Again we eschewed calling an ambulance or going the hospital. We checked out of our motel and retrieved our car. Bev drove almost nonstop to her aunt's home in Oakland, California, where we stayed several days. I lay in a crumpled heap on the passenger side the entire route, unable to drive. I was exhausted. The episodes continued and I was scared. The seizures seemed to strike out of the blue. Maybe they would disappear just as quickly. I tried to tell myself everything would be okay.

I contemplated the unnerving uncertainties. One minute, life was perfect; the next it was in frightening disarray. I didn't know what to expect from one day to the next. Even when I felt strong, I feared what lay ahead.

Back in Corvallis, I was referred to a neurologist who confirmed what Bev had suspected all along. I had epilepsy. Though the doctor couldn't be certain, evidence suggested that I had scarring on the brain from the accident five years earlier. We talked about different treatments.

I didn't want or need to understand the problem.

Just fix it, I told him.

The doctor prescribed a medication that was supposed to prevent seizures. Relieved but still anxious, I turned my thoughts back to skiing and racing.

I assumed I was cured.

———————————

Six years and two months later, in the same town where I had to admit for the first time that I had epilepsy, I stopped in the wee hours of the night so my crew could hook a TENS unit to my foot to combat the pain in my Achilles.

We were due for a crew change, and the two groups, converging briefly, argued again, this time about how to attach the unit. They considered the pocket of my jersey, but the cords weren't long enough. Then they studied my leg. Bev finally told them to tape it to my cycling cleats so it would stay on while I pedaled. I tuned out the crew static and cursed my misfortune.

> *... you're kidding me! ... it's not that far into the race! ... only 500 miles! ... I'm feeling so strong, and now this ... Achilles? I've never had an Achilles problem before ... what's going on? ... how are we going to fix this? ...*

A Transuctaneous Electronic Neuro Stimulator (TENS) unit reduces pain and inflammation by stimulating the nerves beneath the skin. Wires from the unit lead to the electrodes, which are attached at the site of the pain. The unit allows the body to produce healing endorphins and also blocks the pain signals to the brain, masking the symptoms. If it worked, I would no longer feel the pain in my Achilles.

I wanted to believe I was cured, but in my heart I knew better. I'd been in this place before, literally and figuratively.

I pedaled east through the night into the painted deserts and rimrock country of northeastern Arizona on Highway 287, happy to have Flagstaff behind me, leery of the great unknown ahead.

July 29, 1995
Cortez, Colorado

Danny Chew, aka, the "Million Mile Man," leads the pack heading into the Four Corners area, with Rob Kish, Seana Hogan, Muffy Ritz and Tom Davies in pursuit ... Gerry Tatrai, George Thomas and three other riders play leapfrog in north-eastern Arizona and strive to stay in the top 10.

Chapter Three

July 29, 1995

Ultra-marathon cyclists often say that the Race Across America is a metaphor for life. They romanticize the event, giving it a mystical quality that makes it larger than life in their obscure, close-knit world. It consumes riders' thoughts, conversations and time the remainder of the year.

For me, RAAM is more of a microcosm of life. In 11 days, emotions fluctuate wildly. Self-confidence is constantly tested. As soon as one obstacle is overcome, another rears its head. Problem solving is as much a key to finishing as physical strength and psychological stamina.

In two days, I already had known the giddy anticipation of wheeling to the starting line in Irvine, a demoralizing battle against the Mojave's heat, a rebirth in the Arizona mountains and then the unnerving pain in my Achilles near Flagstaff. The highs were exhilarating, the lows debilitating. Compounding those feelings was the isolation. It's just you and your bicycle against the road, the elements and RAAM's demons. So rarely did I see other competitors that I had to constantly remind myself that I was actually in a race.

When the sun rose over the famous monoliths of Monument Valley on the third morning, I was riding high again. A welcome tailwind was nudging me smoothly toward the Four Corners area. Highway 160 stretched like a thin ribbon across the hostile but vivid painted deserts of northeastern Arizona's Navajo country. There wasn't another cyclist or crew in sight, but I didn't mind. Fatigue and pain were offset by a fresh start and brilliant scenery. I savored the idea of pedaling all day in such conditions. My Achilles still hurt, but I managed to pedal through the pain.

> *... this is beautiful country! ... the pinks, the oranges, the purples! ... the sun looks like an enormous fireball ... wish I wasn't so sleepy ... foot still hurts ... can't believe I'm having this much fun ... how far behind am I? ... this road seems to stretch forever ...*

I forced myself to focus on my immediate tasks rather than worrying about the leaders. In my heart, I believed that if I could ride to my abilities I would do fine. The question was whether my body would allow it. Pain never scared me; I knew from experience that I could handle it. Seizures weren't a concern either; medication had those under control. My three primary concerns were the heat, my neck muscles and time. At this point, I had survived the worst of the heat, so now I zeroed in on other worries. I'd heard tales about the dreaded "Shermer Neck," a uniquely RAAM malady in which the neck muscles give out and no longer support the head. It once forced Shermer to quit RAAM just a few hundred miles from the finish. My neck had never been an issue, but then again, my longest solo ride had been California's Furnace Creek 508.

When I wasn't pondering my neck's future, I fretted about my time, because all mystical references to RAAM as a metaphor or a microcosm of life aside, the bottom line is it's a race. You never forget that, no matter how alone you are. Could I shrug off my doubts about remaining within 48 hours of the winner? I kept picturing the other riders pedaling faster and farther, limiting their food and sleep breaks. I had to keep moving, and as a result, also lurking in the recesses of my mind was the specter of RAAM's infamous sleep deprivation and accompanying hallucinations.

While enjoying my morning ride, I continued to wonder what the coming days held.

The conditions were a tease, another sinister element of RAAM. It's difficult to fathom abrupt, dramatic weather changes in a race so steady and slow, but they occur with remarkable frequency and intensity. Sometimes all it takes is a right or left turn. Not long after sunrise, as I cherished the respite from the heat and the pain, I came to a junction where the highway turned sharply into a headwind. Any hopes that this new challenge might be temporary were mitigated by the view. I could see a ribbon of highway stretching for miles and miles across the rimrock country. I hunkered down for another long, hot day.

Soon, despite my protests, my crew began to make me stop every hour to ice my Achilles. Eventually, the pain was severe enough to put the TENS unit back on my leg. I could feel my emotions swinging again. The wind, the heat and the pain were frustrating, but above all I was demoralized. This wasn't as discouraging as the Mojave Desert, but it was perilously close. My Achilles ached, the heat in this thirsty country was oppressive, blood oozed from my nose because of the exertion in the dry air, and I was battling to avoid drifting off to sleep on my bicycle. At least now I knew it was better to stop for breaks than to stubbornly keep going.

My dour mood temporarily changed when we came upon another crew and a cyclist by the side of the road.

> *... who's that? ... it's Gerry Tatrai's crew!*
> *... I'm passing Gerry Tatrai! ... okay, so he's*
> *not riding; I'm still passing him ... I must be*
> *doing okay ... hey, a stop sign ... which way?*
> *... left? ... YES! ... A tailwind! ...*

I spun hard, increasing my pace and elevating my spirits with each passing mile. Gerry Tatrai! I had passed the 31-year-old Australian back in 1993, when I completed RAAM on a relay team and he was pedaling to a solo victory. I always admired his style and his demeanor. As I passed him on my own solo journey, Tatrai and his crew cheered me on. Just like that, RAAM was fun again. I had been on my bike for three days and now I felt recharged as I pedaled briskly in my colorful Serotta uniform. In my focused state, I never did notice Tatrai's crew when they rapidly appeared out of nowhere to flag down my crew less than 30 minutes later.

> *... I love this! ... there's nowhere else I'd*
> *rather be ... here comes my crew ... wonder*
> *what they want ... probably to congratulate me*
> *on my pace ... okay, give them a big smile ...*

The van pulled alongside and Mike leaned out the window.

"Uh, George ... we don't think this is the right way."

I looked at him in utter disbelief as he tried to describe the error. What? I could understand missing a turn in a city or rural area on the congested East Coast, but out here, in the middle of nowhere? As is always the case when a junction nears, the crew had studied the route map and driven ahead to mark the correct turn. Such a mistake seemed unfathomable in this bleak terrain.

"We were supposed to go straight," Mike said.

I remembered the junction. The route went left at an intersection near the Navajo Reservation community of Indian Wells, then took an immediate right. We missed the immediate right turn, meaning we had made a left instead of continuing along the same line. Tatrai's crew had noticed our error and, in an incredible show of sportsmanship, had driven eight miles out of their way to inform us that we were off course. Dejected, I loaded my bike into our van with my stomach in knots. I felt betrayed. I seethed about the lost time. And I was returning to the fierce headwind.

Worst of all, my confidence in my crew was shaken. The people I relied on to take care of me made a grave error. My faith in their navigational skills was shaken. It was especially disheartening that this occurred on Mike's watch. He had become my anchor, a calming force in whom I had developed full confidence in just two days. I tried to concentrate on my race and not worry about the other cyclists, to no avail. The TENS unit buzzed on my leg and my left knee was beginning to ache.

RAAM's rules do allow riders who take wrong turns to be driven back to the course, but precious time was wasted. Returning to the route, I could see riders I had overtaken. As I sat in the van, heading back over the asphalt on which I had just expended energy, I struggled with what to do and say to my crew. I wanted to be polite. For the second time in two days, I had to remind myself that these were friends and family, not a highly trained, professional crew.

... okay, so deal with it ...

On a drizzly September morning in 1981, I was canvassing my newspaper route as usual, with the windows down on both sides of my new Honda Civic so I could throw the *San Antonio Light* onto driveways in either direction.

I'd risen every morning for several years to deliver 650 papers, and it was a job that suited me perfectly. By my senior year in high school, I had become a loner, spending most of my spare hours riding my horse, Ginger, hanging out with my best friend Tracy Williams, or running on cross-country courses I had designed around our San Antonio neighborhood.

I usually enjoyed the early morning serenity. On this day, though, the calm was shattered when I noticed what I thought was a big dog running in front of the car. Sensing that the animal was about to dash in front of me, I hit the brakes. The next thing I knew, the creature had leaped through the passenger window, struggled inside and was in a kicking frenzy trying to get across my lap.

Only then, in the midst of my shock, did I realize that it wasn't a dog frantically trying to escape—it was a full-grown white-tailed deer.

The frightened doe cut her front legs on the door as she burst through and was leaving blood, hair and ripped newspapers in her wake. She kicked me repeatedly in the chest. With one final thrust into my ribs, the deer sprang out the driver's-side window and disappeared into the early morning gloom.

I was a bloody mess, and my ribs ached. Each breath was painful as I finished my route. I soon learned that the cartilage in my rib cage had split.

Great.

I was just beginning what I anticipated would be a promising final cross-country season at Churchill High School. Now I was sure that my entire autumn would be hindered at best, ruined at worst.

The Thomas family at their home in San Antonio, Texas. From left, George, age four, brother Sterling, sister Edith, brother Norman, and mother Edith.

Such travails seemed to be the story of my young life.

When I was three, I tried to run for the first time with my father, Norman, an insurance salesman who was— and is—my first and only true hero. He started jogging in the early 1960s, long before aerobic exercise became trendy. Frequently I joined him for his cool-down walk. I'd take his sweaty hand, feel a close bond and know that I wanted to be just like him.

On the night I finally tried to run with him, I sprinted down the steps, tripped over my feet and landed on my head, rendering myself unconscious. Dad picked me up and, when he realized I wasn't breathing, gave me mouth-to-mouth resuscitation.

The fitness craze swept my family before it swept the nation. They joined the San Antonio Road Runners and we entered fun runs as a group on the weekends. I didn't have a passion for running, but it was what we did, so I participated. It also gave me a taste of success that whetted my appetite. My first ribbon came when I completed four miles of a 10-mile race at age four.

At age six, I tried a 20-mile charity run. I tried to stay with my older brother Sterling and my father, but they soon dropped me. I was alone, hot and tired, and I felt abandoned. At a long bend in the course, I sat on the curb and refused to budge until Sterling and Dad found me. I didn't care about finishing. When they finally arrived and we drove around the curve, there it was, 200 yards away: The finish line. I was suddenly overcome by a sense of failure. Never mind that I had run 19 miles and 800 yards, or that I repeatedly heard how amazing it was that a six-year-old had run so far.

I had quit. I hated the empty feeling and vowed to never, ever do that again.

Generally I was a happy kid with an easy life when I was a youngster. While at Coker Elementary School in San Antonio, I made friends easily and maintained good grades. My parents, Norman and Edith, provided a warm family life and unconditional love. They attended all my sporting events and doted on me. My brothers and sister would watch family movies and joke that I was an only child. In hindsight, perhaps I was too sheltered. As the youngest, I was always shielded from the real world. I became a follower, always one step behind my parents and my siblings.

Any early sense of strong self-esteem abruptly gave way to self-doubt upon entering Eisenhower Middle School in 1975. I was shocked at how poorly I meshed with the other students. The kids were cruel. My out-of-style, hand-me-down clothes were a daily joke. Most of the students used cool backpacks to carry their books; I used one of my dad's battered leather briefcases. Where once I was one of the first to raise my hand in class, I became quiet, introverted and painfully shy, especially around girls. My grades suffered.

I grew to love being alone and I gravitated toward individual sports.

When I did compete with others, I was more comfortable hidden in the middle of the pack, just as fearful of success as afraid of failure. After all, whenever I was close to savoring accomplishments, fate seemed to intervene.

In middle school I struggled to make the cut for meets. Butterflies always churned in my stomach. If I were the slowest runner on our team, I knew there would be many faster runners from other teams. Rather than toeing the starting line fighting to win, I simply hoped to avoid embarrassment.

Then, at age 13, in my last middle school meet I not only made the cut, I was winning a race for the first time

San Antonio Churchill High School Cross Country Team. George is in the back row on the right and Tracy Williams is in the middle row on the right.

in three years. I had less than 220 yards to go in an 880-yard dash. I was in one of two heats and running for all I was worth.

I was amazed. For once, I had overruled all my self-doubts. I felt conspicuous in the lead and sensed everyone's eyes on me, but I wanted more than anything to win. I ignored the footsteps behind me.

Down the final straightaway I came, 100 yards from the finish. I saw the ribbon stretched across the track for the winner to break. I wanted so badly for it to be me. I imagined the entire pack poised to pass, trying to run faster. I was sure I'd be passed.

I wasn't.

I broke the tape, looked back and saw that no one was within 25 yards. My teammates ran to congratulate me. I was so happy I was dizzy. First place! I went to the center of the field to await the award ceremony, eager to receive my first and last middle school ribbon. I was giddy as the announcer began to call out names in descending order, starting with sixth place. I'd won my heat so convincingly that my teammates and I were certain I'd placed well and perhaps even won.

The names rang out: Fifth, fourth, third. I still hadn't heard my name. Second place … still no George Thomas. I couldn't believe it! I had won!

I listened excitedly for the announcement for first.

It wasn't me.

I went numb. My teammates wandered off. Not only did I not win, I hadn't even placed. I was left alone with my disappointment and hurt.

For the next three years I continued to run nondescript races in high school, usually finishing in the middle of the varsity pack.

My senior year, I believed I was finally primed for the success that had proved so elusive. Then the deer leaped into my lap on that drizzly morning in San Antonio.

Running was excruciating that entire autumn. My ribs were always taped, so breathing was a chore. San Antonio's late-summer heat was merciless.

My cross-country season was solid nonetheless. I finished fourth at districts, but then dropped out at the regional because of the pain. Even worse, it was clear that the pain wasn't going away any time soon.

I had two options: Quit, or deal with it.

For three months, I ran with the pain. My spring track season was a bust. I would hit a certain speed and couldn't go any faster. Afterward, I forced myself to run 10Ks and fared well. At one time I ran a 34:59 and finished in the top five in a big road race in San Antonio. I couldn't sprint, but I could hold a pace over 10K.

It was a source of pride that I had learned to just deal with it.

I never imagined that eventually it would become a crutch.

Familiar feelings of self-doubt crept into my psyche as I sat in the back of the van on that lonely road in northeastern Arizona. Gerry Tatrai and his crew were long gone. Once back on course, I could see three riders pedaling toward me over my shoulder. I felt the pressure of the pursuit. As we approached a turn on a narrow two-lane road, crew cars began to pass.

I had been riding so well, at the top of my game, and now this.

... how could my crew have done this to me? ... three riders closing in ... how did they catch me so fast? ... I was so strong yesterday...they're coming so fast! ... gotta get moving ... okay, stop thinking about the crew and concentrate ... can't concentrate ... darned headwinds ... darned Achilles ... they're passing ...

Seeing the competition is a bittersweet feeling, especially when it arrives from behind. The company and camaraderie provide a welcome respite. Then you remember: It's a race. At first pleasantries are exchanged when a car or van pulls off the road in the middle of the nowhere. Yet in the back of your mind you know that the crew is measuring your progress. You know this because your crew is doing the same—or at least you hope so. At this point, I was sure the other crews were better equipped, more savvy, more knowledgeable and better navigators.

Three riders passed when I was pedaling off-course. Despite my pain and frustration, or perhaps because of it, I slowly regained ground. We played leapfrog with a Japanese camera crew, which took a liking to me. They drove ahead of their rider to get footage of us.

By late afternoon, I was laboring again. I could see classic desert thunderstorms in the distance, their clouds rising like purple towers over the mesas. Normally I love riding in the rain, but the previous day I had spilled water on the leg bearing the TENS unit. It felt like fire crawling up the back of my leg and into my head. I wondered if the stimulation of the nerves might trigger a seizure.

I cringed at the thought of raindrops pelting me.

... better stop ... no, gotta keep going ...
Colorado isn't far ... it would feel so good to get
into another state ... can't believe I feel so good
... temperature is comfortable ... but these
headwinds are brutal! ...

I looked down at the computer mounted on my handlebars. It registered 8 mph. I thought I had been making progress toward Colorado, some 80 miles away, but at 8 mph I realized I was still 10 hours out. Normally in 10 hours I'd cover close to 200 miles. As the sun dropped over the same pink and red mesas behind me, my crew started playing books on tape over the speakers. I thought this would distract me from the grueling pace, but instead it slowed me. I couldn't hear the words well so I'd cock my head to the side. With music, I could sing along, but a book required too much concentration and created aggravation.

As night fell, the storm sidestepped me and dissipated. The wind stopped and I was surrounded by pitch black. I picked up my pace. The lights on my bike and the trailing van were like a beacon gliding across the rolling desert at 18-20 mph. I was eager to reach Colorado because I'd also ridden well on this section as part of my first RAAM relay team in 1993, but Arizona was dragging on forever. I saw the lights of a town ahead, thinking it was Cortez, Colorado, only to be discouraged to learn that it was Teec Nos Pas, Arizona.

A large skunk appeared on the side of the road on a steep hill and seemed to keep pace with me. It lifted its tail as if to offer a warning for my labored intrusion. I doubted I could pedal fast enough to outrun him, and in my beleaguered state, I frankly didn't care. Go ahead and shoot.

... wow, I feel good, but I must be going soooo slow ...

I was more concerned about other apparitions on the road. Giant tarantulas, spiders and scorpions scurried under my pedals. They were everywhere. The sensation was strange, but it did have a benefit: It kept me from stopping because there was no way I was going to put my feet down. In the morning, after a sleep break, the tarantulas, spiders and scorpions would revert to tar blobs. I was having my first hallucinations brought on by sleep deprivation.

Finally, I passed through the Four Corners area into Colorado and could see Cortez in the distance, a glittering jewel in the darkness. Eric, a former Colorado resident, started telling me about the state's history over the PA and said he'd point out landmarks. Trouble was, it was pitch dark. I was hurting and tired and asked my crew for the long sleep break in Cortez that Bruce and I had agreed upon earlier in the day. I stopped, took a shower, savored a massage, crawled into bed and slept through sunrise.

When I awoke after a two-hour nap, Mike and I were eager to hit the pavement. I was looking forward to climbing Wolf Creek Pass, the pinnacle of RAAM. I was hurting, but I felt refreshed and the temperatures were perfect.

We looked for the rest of the crew, but they were nowhere in sight. Apparently they left to shop and do laundry while Mike and I slept, a task my parents and aunt could've handled if only my crew had communicated well.

I sat in the motel room and fumed. Mike was angry and embarrassed.

"I'll go on by myself," I said.

"No," Mike said. "We don't want you to get lost again."

I tried to go back to sleep, but couldn't. So I fidgeted in the motel room for another wasted hour, thinking about the other riders out there putting distance between them and me.

Another day, another obstacle.

I would just have to deal with it.

July 30, 1995
Wolf Creek Pass, Colorado

As RAAM reaches its first significant milestone—tower-ing Wolf Creek Pass—Danny Chew is keeping Seana Hogan, Rob Kish and Muffy Ritz at arm's length ... Dieter Weik and Tom Davies have dropped back, but are still ahead of Beat Gfeller and Gerry Tatrai ... George Thomas is in a three-way battle with Reed Finfrock and Rickey Wray Wilson, catching Finfrock at the summit after trailing by nearly an hour at the base.

Chapter Four

July 30, 1995

My crew finally arrived with clean laundry, fresh food and gallons of purified water, and as I began the transition from the desolate Four Corners area into the rugged San Juan Mountains of southwestern Colorado, my spirits were buoyant again.

A RAAM benchmark lay just ahead: 10,850-foot Wolf Creek Pass, the highest point in the race. I was also refreshed from my stay at the Comfort Inn in Cortez. Even more significant, Mike had read my discouragement as I pedaled between Cortez and Durango. Just as I had hit another nadir and began openly questioning whether I could finish within 48 hours of the winner, the van pulled alongside and Mike extended his arm out the window. He was holding a cell phone.

"George," he said, "you have a call."

I looked at him quizzically, took the phone and wearily said, "Hello."

"Daddy!" squealed the three-year-old voice on the other end.

It was Meredith. Mike, seeing I needed an emotional boost, had called my daughter in Corvallis. The perfect tonic. After a five-minute chat with Meredith, my batteries were recharged.

Moments later, we passed a motor home parked under a shade tree. Paul Solon of Corte Madera, California, and his crew were inside. He had withdrawn from the

Three-year-old Meredith sits on George's sister Edith's lap next to George and his father Norman. George had just completed the 1994 San Diego, Calif. to Charleston, S.C. PAC Tour.

*George pedals hard up the steep grade to Wolf Creek Pass,
east of Pagosa Springs, Colorado.*

race. Perhaps I was holding up better than I thought. A
few minutes later, we passed fellow rookie Kaname Sakurai
and his crew, also parked by the road. I waved. They smiled,
cheered and snapped pictures.

I had again put a crew gaffe behind me as I pedaled
purposefully through Pagosa Springs toward Wolf Creek.
I was eager for the challenge and knew what lay ahead. I
had crested the pass for my relay teams in 1993 and 1994.
As I left Durango, dozens of motorcyclists passed me heading west. I waved as they gave me the thumbs-up signal.

My newfound strength helped me accept the omni-
present pains I had accumulated 1,000 miles into the race.
I couldn't sit long because the bones in my rump were
tender and my saddle sores were oozing. At least the TENS
unit was camouflaging the pain in my Achilles, so I could
get out of the saddle. That was the only relief. When I sat,

I squirmed in a futile attempt to find comfort. The crew found some large pads to insert in my shorts, but by now I was resigned to the reality that every part of my body would hurt the rest of the way. I finally told myself to quit whining.

"Your form doesn't look as good as it did yesterday," Bruce observed.

... no kidding ...

At the base of Wolf Creek I was told that I was 40 minutes behind Reed "The Flamingo" Finfrock, a 48-year-old rookie from Lindsay, California. My adrenaline spurted. Wolf Creek Pass is the first of four major milestones during RAAM, a mystical pinnacle on par with the race's ceremonial midway point in Slapout, Oklahoma, the crossing of the Mississippi River, and reaching the Georgia state line. Just being at the base evoked fond images of my previous two RAAMs.

My natural high was abetted by my pursuit of Finfrock and the gorgeous pine-scented scenery. "Love Drive" by the Scorpions and Eric Johnson's "Cliffs of Dover" blared from the loudspeakers atop the support van, spurring me on. Tourists who stopped for the breathtaking views cheered as I inched past them at overlooks on the ascent. I pretended that they were lining the route to cheer for me, as if this was the Tour de France and I was in the Alps. I saw my dad talking to strangers and could read the amazement in their eyes as I pedaled past. *He's going from where to where? On a bicycle!?*

At the summit of the 10-mile climb I was surprised to see Reed in his pink Lycra and flamingo helmet, a trademark ever since he first rode in California's Furnace Creek 508, where competitors are identified by animal names instead of numbers. I was thrilled. I had erased his 40-

minute lead in less than two hours. I stopped briefly in the cool mountain air to change into warm clothes for the descent. The sun was beginning to dip behind the San Juans to the west. A good day was about to become a great night.

Reed took off ahead of me, signaling the start of a unique RAAM competition/companionship that would last for days and seal a bond and kinship that only participants in an ultra-event like this can comprehend. I climbed into my saddle and sped down the highway, exceeding 40 mph on the twisting descent into the heart of the Rocky Mountains.

> *… what a transition … from sunny and puffy white clouds to overcast and dark … shouldn't have stopped so long at the top … 40 mph? … go faster … last time I was here I did 55-60 … this isn't good …*

Repeatedly, I had already been shown how cruelly fleeting prosperity is in RAAM. I couldn't imagine the race becoming any more diabolical than it had been in the Mojave Desert, or at Flagstaff, or in the Four Corners area.

I was wrong. With no warning, my fortunes plummeted almost as quickly as I descended from Wolf Creek Pass.

The first salvo from the RAAM gods was a construction zone that slowed my pace to a crawl, jarring my tender bones, muscles and tendons. Rain began to fall and temperatures dropped. At the tiny community of South Fork, I again passed Reed, who was laboring under the duress. Any thrill I had over catching a fellow rookie was offset by my own agony. Grinding along at less than 10 mph compounded my pain. The aching in my saddle sores,

In high school, one of George's favorite pastimes was riding his horse, Vibes, with his best friend Tracy Williams.

Achilles and sore knee was even more acute. Worse, in the stark darkness of south-central Colorado, I for the first time felt an overwhelming sense of loneliness as I rode in the headlights of the night crew's van toward Alamosa.

> *... wow, this is really cruel ... can't be-*
> *lieve the race people are making me do this ...*
> *how can I feel so bad after feeling so good? ...*

At Alamosa, I summoned my crew and said I needed to stop. Maybe a sleep break would change my attitude. I staggered into the van and probably fell asleep before my head hit the pillow. I was eager for a fitful nap, yet in what seemed like milliseconds, Sabra was shaking me, trying to rouse me.

"Why are you waking me up?" I asked, groggily.

"It's been an hour," she replied.

I looked at her in disbelief. I felt like I had blinked. I questioned Sabra, thinking my crew was playing with my head to keep me moving. They showed me their watches. One hour. I lay there, immobilized. I was as tired as I could ever remember. My body hurt. I was sick of slimy mayo sandwiches, liquid foods and vitamins. Nearly 2,000 miles of unforgiving RAAM pavement lay ahead. I wanted to close my eyes and sleep for a week.

For the first time, RAAM's feared "quit factor" was taking hold of my psyche.

As a youngster, and even into my early adulthood, I was a searcher lurking in the middle of the pack, always following somebody—if not my father, then my brothers, my friends or people in a race. I wasn't so much afraid of academic and athletic failure as I was fearful of success.

I saw my successes in running as a genetic gift from my parents. To ensure that I'd always have an excuse for not winning, I scarcely trained except on my occasional solo runs on my neighborhood courses. When I started riding a bicycle, I never worked out diligently. I had dreams, but rarely did I have the desire or perseverance to pursue them seriously.

I was close to my parents, and I had one close friend, Tracy Williams, with whom I'd ridden horses since high school. Tracy was my confidante, my buddy and the one person outside my family I trusted most. We rode horses or my motorcycle almost every day and shared our most private feelings. I was saddened when she went off to college at Texas A&M in 1981.

That same year, I graduated from San Antonio's Churchill High School and considered attending Stephen

F. Austin State University in Nacogdoches, Texas. I talked myself out of it. I was making $900 a month working two hours per day and living at home. I had a little red Fiat sports car and a motorcycle that had replaced my horse. I had plenty of money, lots of time and little responsibility. I was content. Instead of leaving home, I enrolled at the University of Texas's branch campus in San Antonio, mostly because it seemed the thing to do. I had no idea what my major would be.

It probably was a mistake. I never felt as if I made a life transition. It was more like going to a bigger high school. My life continued to be little more than delivering newspapers, attending school and occasionally riding or running.

Two years after starting at Texas-San Antonio, I had my first serious girlfriend, Gayle, a fellow student. Gayle brought some focus to my life. She suggested I pursue a career in teaching. With my sports background, I was naturally drawn to physical education. I agreed. I was embarrassed about playing games like foursquare with kids when serious students were walking by on campus, but at least I now had a goal.

Gayle wasn't keen on having a college boyfriend who had a paper route, so I added a job at Foot Locker, where I showed up to work in those double-knit black pants and a striped referee's shirt. My schedule exhausted me, and I began to think I was missing out on life experiences. All I did was deliver papers, work and go to class, where I was a mediocre student earning a 2.3 grade point average. I rarely studied because I had no time for homework. I was so tired from getting up early and working night shifts that I would literally nod off in class, once waking up in big puddle of drool on my desk.

A job as a phys-ed teacher was waiting for me upon graduation, but it wasn't an exciting prospect. Though I liked teaching and enjoyed helping coach the track team, I didn't have a passion for either.

So I planned a cross-country motorcycle trip instead.

In the meantime, I continued to ride my bicycle sparingly and entered a few small races in the citizen's category. The results were unspectacular.

In the spring of 1984, Sterling and Sabra asked if I'd be interested in joining them on a team in the annual Spenco 500, a relay race in the hill country around Austin. To that point, my longest solo ride had been 50 miles. A typical training ride covered 10. Under Spenco rules, each cyclist has one ride, meaning I would have to cover 100 miles nonstop.

Sure, I said.

Sterling, Sabra and John Franknecht were all accomplished triathletes, and our fifth rider, named Debbie, who would later meet us on the course and ride 60 miles, was also ultra-fit. For a crew vehicle, we secured an old Ford van with a cut-out roof and a bed in the rear.

We drove to Waco and I nervously awaited the start. Some big names were present, including three-time Olympian and Ironman winner John Howard, as well as a few pros. I went first for our team because I was the "experienced" cyclist.

The gun sounded and I found myself in the lead. I couldn't believe it when I looked over my shoulder and saw the entire field 100 yards behind. Little did I know. It was a scorching Texas day, and before long it seemed like every rider had caught me. I brought two water bottles but didn't use them. I wanted to conserve. My mouth was dry, making it difficult to chew and almost impossible to swallow. The crew had disappeared. At mile 60, I saw Sterling by the side of the road, and he gave me some figs. Ugh. I sipped from my bottle, which produced hot water. Ugh. I had no choice. I had to eat the figs for nutrition, but they only made me thirstier. Soon I ran out of water.

I was in serious trouble.

Thirsty, sore and on the verge of bonking, I saw a motor home on the side of the road, rode past and pulled a U-turn on my bike. I knocked on the door and was greeted by a pleasant and understanding fellow who gave me water and let me lie down in air-conditioned bliss. My team had no idea where I was. I felt guilty; if I had been in shape, I could've stopped at the motor home, asked for water and got moving again.

Soon there was a knock on the door, and it was Sterling, who saw my bike on the side of the trailer. I'd ridden 90 miles. Sabra had taken over, riding 115. John did 130. Debbie did her 60 and Sterling covered the last 120, getting us into fourth place.

I felt terrible. I hadn't carried my weight and I'd blown the race for us. I vowed to redeem myself.

A week after Spenco, I entered the Wildflower 100, a tour that was my first century ride. It was cool and a light rain was falling. I rode with a small group for 50 miles, and my parents played leapfrog with me, providing plenty of food and liquids when they'd pass. I finished and earned a beautiful Texas-shaped plaque for being "The First to Finish Their First Century."

The next Thursday, brimming with confidence, I entered a San Antonio Bicycling Club time trial. I was passed by a few riders and had a poor race, but I had fun anyway. Life was good. My motorcycle journey loomed. I was about to enjoy the freedom of the road.

In the spring of 1984, Tracy returned. I was eager to catch up with her and share the plans of my trip. I invited her for a ride and motored over to her house on Patricia Street in San Antonio to pick her up. It was Mother's Day eve.

I exchanged pleasantries with Tracy's mother and then walked outside to where my motorcycle was parked. I had two helmets, a top-of-the-line model that I usually wore and an older one I gave to passengers. On this day, I planned to give the good one to Tracy, but for whatever reason as I walked outside I put on the newer one, which covered my face and my Adam's apple and was made of stronger material.

If not for that momentary lapse, I'd surely be dead.

Moments later, I was lying in the road, amid a flood of gyrating lights, surrounded by hands, dark faces and strange voices. And I'll never forget the pain. Every inch of my body was throbbing. I felt as if a huge middle line-backer had just tackled me. What happened? Had I had run a stop sign? Had I hit a rock? What about Tracy? I remember feeling relief when told she was okay.

Initially, I swore as loud as I could. Then I blacked out, only to wake again in the ambulance on the way to the hospital. I knew right then that my summer plans were over. My life had changed forever.

As I stretched out in a catatonic state in the van outside of Alamosa, Colorado, I pondered the ramifications of quitting.

I knew Bev wouldn't mind. Her battles with Bruce were difficult enough; watching her husband suffer was testing her fortitude. Little did I know that several times already she had considered buying a one-way Greyhound bus ticket for Corvallis. I wasn't certain how the rest of the crew would feel, but I knew of the mounting friction between Bruce's by-the-book day squad and Bev's more relaxed night crew.

None of them could possibly comprehend the triple whammy of pain, sleep deprivation and physical and psychological exhaustion. Nobody could understand what I had been through in 1,000 miles. All I wanted was a hot shower, a real meal and a bed.

Yet as I considered packing up my Serotta and turning the vans around, a familiar feeling jarred me. The extreme pain, fatigue and frustration elicited images of the accident 11 years earlier and the subsequent rehabilitation.

I remembered how much I hurt then. I remembered how discouraging and painful it was to learn to use muscle, tendons and bones again. I remembered that always there were but two options: Quit or keep going.

Lie in bed all day and pity myself. Or walk again.

Lie in the van all the way back to Corvallis. Or walk with pride again.

I had been at a defining moment in my life and forged ahead.

Now I was at a defining moment in RAAM, which as painful as it was still paled compared to learning to walk again.

> *... do you hurt badly enough that you can look back at this moment and say it was bad enough to quit? ... if you quit, you'll never know if you could've fought through it and finished ... is it worth it? ...you've hurt worse than this ... nobody's making you do this ... you CHOSE to be here ... you knew there would be highs and lows ... remember? ... so what else are you going to do? ... you're out in the middle of nowhere ... either sit in the van and do nothing and lose time or get on the bike and move ... all right ... stop whining and get back on the bike ...*

To say that my solo pep talk instantly reinvigorated me would be disingenuous. The fourth night was easily the longest. It seemed unusually black. I yearned for passing cars to break up the monotony, but they were rare in the high valleys of southern Colorado. I didn't even see Reed. I staggered uphill, plodded on the flats and couldn't muster the energy to pedal on descents. Approaching the base of 9,413-foot La Veta Pass west of Walsenburg, I could see the lights of a lone car that seemed miles above me.

> *… uhhhh, why are those stars moving? …*
> *no way … are those HEADLIGHTS? … I have a*
> *long way to go …*

I barely remember the ride up La Veta. On the way down, I started to get drowsy and hallucinate. I saw several hippopotamuses lying on their sides along the road. I blinked and looked again. Two of the hippos turned into horses. Usually I love the solitude of riding at night, but this was painful.

When the sun finally rose above Cuchara Pass on Day 5, my spirits lifted with it. The new day magically brought a new energy, tapped from a reservoir I was just beginning to understand. I still don't know where it comes from, but I breathed deeply, grateful that I hadn't let myself quit the previous night. The lessons from my accident rehabilitation 11 years earlier had carried into RAAM. I would always have highs and lows, and no matter how miserable I felt, it would pass.

Quitting would never be an option again.

July 31, 1995
Springfield, Colorado

Danny Chew, the 1994 Rookie of the Year, leaves the mountains and passes through Time Station 27 in Balko, Oklahoma, 261 miles ahead of George Thomas. He is averaging 14.1 mph and 337 miles per day ... Seana Hogan, three-time women's champion, is 20 miles behind Chew ... Rob Kish is two miles behind her, just ahead of Muffy Ritz ... Dieter Weik is 68 miles back of the lead, Beat Gfeller is 103 and Gerry Tatrai is 172 ... Rickey Wray Wilson is one mile behind Thomas and Reed Finfrock is 37 miles back ... Terry Wilson has dropped out because of a loss of eyesight, and C. J. Ong, Jr. and David Kees have quit because of dehydration.

Chapter Five

July 31, 1995

The ride to the top of Cuchara Pass brought new hope and excitement on a bright new day.

From Cuchara it was all downhill to Savannah. The descent on the eastern slope of the Rockies would give way to the rolling Great Plains of Colorado and Oklahoma, which in turn would gradually slope toward the Atlantic—with a different type of climbing ahead in the Ozarks and Appalachians.

The plan was to switch permanently at the summit of Cuchara to my titanium bicycle, which was built for speed. In the heart of the Rockies, I rode a stripped-down bicycle with lighter wheels for climbing. My Serotta had fancy wheels, was more aerodynamic and had aerobars pointing straight out from my handlebars so that I could ride lower and more comfortably for longer distances. I hadn't been on it since the western slope of Wolf Creek Pass, because even though the Rockies did have flat stretches, we weren't confident about reading the terrain. We wanted to be careful with speed, especially at night.

At Cuchara, I was confident I could finally let my hair down. Some long descents loomed. I felt strong and reasonably healthy again. I was eager to see eastern Colorado and Oklahoma, which I remembered fondly from Team RAAM. My two crews were still at odds, but they only periodically crossed paths. The previous night's agony was a distant memory.

I was happy to see Mike standing alongside the titanium bicycle at the summit. I disembarked, took a short break and mentally prepared to descend aboard my new ride while my crew put the climbing bike on top of the van. My eagerness was tempered by the strange position of the aerobars extending from the handlebars. They were pointing almost straight up. This wasn't the way they were adjusted just before Wolf Creek Pass.

> *… why are the aerobars different? … they look like goat horns … guess Mike knows what he's doing, but this bike looks stupid …*

The impact was immediate. I couldn't rest comfortably on the aerobars, which allow riders to rest their elbows on pads while tucking low in an aerodynamic position. They're especially useful in headwinds. But when I leaned forward in the tuck position I felt stress on my neck. I could barely hold my head up. I reached speeds better than 60 mph on the descent, passing Ricky Wray Wilson on the way down, yet all I could think about was my neck's heaviness. I began to ponder the RAAM malady I dreaded more than all others—more than the heat, more than the climbs, more than the saddle sores, more than all the myriad aches and pains combined.

> *… oh no … not this …*

I had read about "Shermer Neck." RAAM cyclists joke about it, prepare for it, fear it. Riding in crouched positions for 10 or 11 consecutive days, the neck is given a challenging task. On aerobars, the rider's back is almost parallel to the pavement, with the neck holding up 25 pounds of dead weight in an almost peek-a-boo position so that you can see the road ahead. Most of the strain is in the back of the neck, just above where the muscles meet the shoulders.

"Shermer Neck" was christened in 1983, when race cofounder Michael Shermer began to experience pain 2,400 miles into the second Race Across America. Shermer tried to keep going, using one hand to steer his bicycle and the other to prop up his head. With 700 miles to go, after riding only 10 miles in two hours, he dropped out. A legend was born. Nearly one-third of all RAAM participants have neck problems despite every effort to prevent them. I knew that many riders wore neck collars, but I also was aware of how miserable they were. It's so notorious that the race offered a prize in 1995 for the rider who suffered from the most neck pain.

I remembered thinking before the start that if I could choose to avoid one RAAM pitfall, "Shermer Neck" would be it. We brought inflatable plastic neck collars just in case, hoping we'd never need them.

For more than 1,200 miles, while nearly every other part of my body ached and groaned, I had avoided neck issues. Now, as I barreled toward the Great Plains and my next break in Trinidad, Colorado, I was yearning more for a massage than sleep.

> *... wow, my head is heavy ... why did Mike adjust the aerobars? ... they were working fine ... can't wait to get to Trinidad ...*

I don't remember the ride in the back of an ambulance from Tracy's house to Methodist Hospital in San Antonio, but my mom surely does. Though I was bloodied and broken and nearly in shock, I was lucid enough to speak. She still talks about the words that coursed from her little Mr. Pure Boy's mouth. I never swore, but she insists that I cursed all the way to the hospital.

She said it was the most beautiful sound she's ever heard.

Only later did I learn what happened: A car driven by a woman who allegedly was drunk careened around the 35-mph bend in front of Tracy's home at 50 mph. We never saw her. Tracy heard the impact and turned in time to see me hurtling head over heels through the air. Her mother heard the screeching tires and a loud bang. Without turning to look, she immediately walked inside and dialed 9-1-1.

My brother Norman, a lawyer, later showed me pictures. I could see where my body hit the car's bumper, my butt caved in the hood, my head knocked out the windshield on the passenger side and my body crushed the roof. Another dent was visible where my head hit the trunk. If there had been a passenger in the car, he or she most likely would've been killed by my impact.

I landed on a curb, 190 feet away. The driver was unscathed. To this day, we don't know where she is or what happened to her.

At the hospital, I was taken to a dark room, where a male nurse began cutting off my pants. It's amazing the silly thoughts that come to mind at traumatic times. My first reaction was, "These are my favorite pants!" Then, "I'm still a virgin! I waited all these years for the right person ... why?"

I wasn't aware of the surrounding chaos. I only remember hating the shots of the blood thinner Heparin in my stomach. One night a beautiful nurse came in to give me a shot in stomach. I looked her square in the eye and said, "I love you." I don't think she ever came back.

When I was fully coherent for the first time, my head ached and I couldn't move my left leg. Barely touching the tip of my toes was like getting my legs whacked with a sledgehammer. The doctors eventually gave me a laundry list of casualties. Several ribs were broken or cracked. My hands were shredded. I had an indentation in my left calf from the car's bumper, making it impossible to see where the shinbone ended and the muscle began. My right knee was badly damaged. My ankle was broken. My left foot was pointed down like I was on tiptoes. Both feet were immobile. Most frightening of all, my left leg had blood clots that could force amputation to save my life.

It seemed the only part of me to escape unscathed was my head. The doctors were amazed. Even though I was unconscious or semiconscious for hours, immediate tests revealed no neurological damage.

After a few days, I managed to move around stiffly on my shriveled body. My dad kept coaxing me out of bed, but I was motivated to walk by my desire to get to the bathroom. My physical therapists said they'd never seen anyone so eager to see them.

After eight days, I left the hospital. My dad wheeled me up to the house and carried me up the steps. I was wearing a brace on my leg that I'd remove at night simply for a snippet of freedom. One night I dreamed I was up and walking, and apparently my legs were moving. I woke up screaming because my right knee locked up.

My dad hired a physical therapist who first hooked me up to electrodes, then had me begin lifting small weights. I began to get a small range of motion back in my knees. The weight would help pull my leg down and the electrical device would help lift it up. My legs were so atrophied that my quads were virtually nonexistent.

The toll wasn't just physical. I had been going out with Gayle for 18 months, and at one point we were engaged. We were on again, off again, and the day of the accident she was upset because I had scheduled a bike race on Mother's Day instead of going to church with her.

She offered little support during rehabilitation and eventually broke up with me.

My turning point came when I began to get the motion back in my knees, about two months after the accident. A friend brought an indoor trainer for my bicycle to the house. Every day I'd ride it in front of the television.

In August 1984, three months after the accident and on the day that Alexi Grewal won gold in the road race at the Los Angeles Olympics, I took my bicycle off the trainer and rode it outdoors for the first time. I pedaled two miles around the neighborhood. There were some big hills and I was terrified of cars, but I made it. Part of me thought, "Gawd, I had to put out all that effort for two miles!" But another part of me was proud for accomplishing the feat.

I rode every day after that, gradually adding distance. In September, I entered a triathlon. I was surprisingly strong on the bike and run, but I couldn't swim because I couldn't keep my legs up. I would bob to the bottom of the pool and back up. I finished third in my division.

It wasn't much of a triathlon, but it motivated me to enter the San Antonio Bicycle Racing Club city championships that same month. I shaved my legs for the first time, using a Bic disposable razor. The night before the race I couldn't sleep because my legs itched.

I was excited. I still couldn't walk well, so being on my bicycle offered me a sense of freedom. I was so excited that at the beginning of the prologue—a time trial on a hill that was about a mile long—I disregarded the advice of a person at the starting line and began in my biggest chain ring. I took off on a little downhill, then came around a corner and started up a super-steep hill. I made it in my big chain ring, but I was bogging down and the hill was getting steeper. I thought, "Wow, I'd better shift," but my bike wouldn't shift. Riders passed me one by one.

I lost five minutes to the leader in my class in one mile. I was so embarrased I thought about quitting. But my parents kept saying, "You can't quit," and inside I knew I couldn't either.

That night I was miserable from the itching and even worse from the humiliation, but when I woke up the next morning I felt strong entering the criterium, a circular course typically less than a mile long with sharp corners. I broke away with the lead pack of five and we started putting some time on the guys who were so far ahead of me the previous day. I had a mechanical problem with my bicycle, but I got a free lap under the rules, got a new wheel and was put back with the break group. I did well despite a one-minute penalty for a mechanical that should've been taken care of before the race.

And that afternoon I won a time trial.

My itchy legs notwithstanding, I'd never felt better about myself. I was racing in the citizen's class, but even among the best riders my time was in the top three. I also had made up a ton of time. The next morning I went out with the pack on the road race and finished fourth overall.

Afterward, the public-address announcer handed me a little trophy and said, "Hey, this guy couldn't walk three months ago!"

Being slow in a race or having a disastrous result, either of which would have caused me to consider quitting before the accident, would never faze me again. I would always be motivated to do even better.

As an athlete, ironically, the accident made me better. It changed my outlook. It gave me a toughness I never had. I realized I could absorb a lot of pain.

Until the accident, my approach to bicycle racing had been lethargic. I had no plans for a future in the sport. I didn't train. I had no idea what real pain was about and wasn't eager to find out. I couldn't fathom shaving my legs, which serious cyclists do to care for road rash and to make massages easier.

My outlook on bicycling and life had changed in front of Tracy's house in San Antonio, in the hospital and during my physical therapy.

I was losing interest in school at Texas-San Antonio. I was questioning my choice of majors. The only saving grace was my primary professor, George Colfer, a runner and cyclist who shared my interest in those sports. He offered me direction and encouragement. By the summer of 1985, I had earned a Category 3 rating from the United States Cycling Federation.

After his recovery from the accident, George found
fulfillment as a ski instructor at Oregon's Mt. Bachelor.

I was getting antsy, so I transferred to Stephen F. Austin State University in Nacogdoches, about 300 miles northeast of San Antonio. I changed my major to something I thought I'd enjoy, communications, and was hired as news director at KTBC-FM, a tiny radio station. I loved it. One of my first stories was about Donna Marie Bennett, a nine-month-old local girl who needed a liver transplant. I organized a 430-mile solo bicycle tour to raise awareness and funds for Donna Marie.

My budding career as a news reporter ended abruptly when I saw my first dead person. While covering a ditch cave-in, I saw a man's arm sticking out of the ground. I was appalled at the way my colleagues crowded around and gawked. All I could think about was how the man had gotten up that morning like every other. I wondered if he ate breakfast, said good-bye to his wife and kids, and told them what time he'd be home that night.

I realized then I could never be a reporter. I switched to morning deejay at the radio station and hosted a discussion show affiliated with the university. I also taught entry-level speech.

In December 1985, I visited Oregon for the first time and was mesmerized by the scenic beauty. After graduating from Stephen F. Austin in May 1986, I returned to the Northwest that winter and took a part-time job at Hoodoo Ski Bowl in the Cascade Mountains west of Bend. Hoodoo made me a full-time ski instructor and paid me $5 an hour. I started graduate school at Stephen F. Austin in 1987, but when I called Hoodoo to see if they needed help during Christmas break they told me they could use me if I hired on full-time for the season. I made a knee-jerk decision to quit school and become a ski instructor. It was after my move to Oregon that I met Bev on a blind date while rock climbing.

I never gave much thought to the occasional dizzy spells that came and went and the extreme fatigue I'd feel when I rode. I always figured it was the 4,000-foot altitude of Oregon's Santiam Pass, where Hoodoo is located. The dizzy spells would pass and I thought I'd eventually adjust to the thin, dry air.

I was having too much fun to worry about the episodes. Skiing was a blast. Bev and I were dating and planning a life together. Oregon was beautiful.

The dizzy spells sometimes were severe enough to prevent me from skiing, but I ignored them.

Until it was too late, and I was lying on that bathroom floor in Flagstaff.

Our original plan called for a three-hour stop in Trinidad. With a two and a half-hour nap, I could spend 30 minutes on the massage table, with Rena's hands working over my neck. I hoped that an ounce of prevention would provide a cure in the old mining town that serves as a gateway between the Rockies and the Plains.

As I left Trinidad, my head was feeling even heavier. I soon stopped and signaled for my crew. They pumped up the bladder-shaped neck collars, which we thought would be provide support and comfort. They did neither. And they were pumped up so tight it was difficult to eat. I could barely open my mouth and chew. The more I rode, the more discouraged I became. I expected to make up time in the flats near Springfield, Colorado, but I had to sit upright to keep my head up. The winds blew straight from the east, directly into my face, chest and torso. I could've pedaled briskly despite the headwinds because nothing else hurt at the moment, but I couldn't get down out of the wind.

Like my dizzy spells nearly a decade earlier, I tried to ignore my growing neck pain as I pedaled in darkness into stiff winds across the high plains of eastern Colorado. Except for this one nagging concern, this was a memorable part of the race. I was excited to return to Oklahoma, even if I had to have my left hand under my chin, holding up my head. When we left Springfield, Colo., and crossed the border just west of Boise City, my crew cranked up big band music on the loudspeakers.

My crews were getting along, though they were still arguing about how to best feed me. Bruce and the day crew wanted to keep me on liquids. Bev and the night crew wanted me to have more fat for energy. I resisted eating and drinking on the bike, so they were worried about my caloric intake. They were willing to break Bruce's regimen and gave me whatever solid foods I would eat. At sunrise in Guymon, Oklahoma, we stopped at McDonald's, where I took a bath in the sink and my crew gave me a delicious bacon, egg and cheese biscuit. The crews argued briefly about feeding me McDonald's, but they were at least lighthearted about it.

All that breeziness was about to change dramatically. It started to rain, and when I boarded my bicycle again my neck was hurting worse than ever. I had lost my faith and confidence in Mike, my right-hand man for the first 1,500 miles, and I was blaming him for my neck woes. I realized I might be riding for days, perhaps the remainder of the race, with my hand on my chin. What a demoralizing prospect.

… all right, this is it …

August 1, 1995
Slapout, Oklahoma

In the rolling plains of the Oklahoma panhandle, Rob Kish has overtaken Danny Chew and Seana Hogan at Guthrie, 1,617 miles into RAAM and 287 miles ahead of George Thomas ... Muffy Ritz is fourth ... Rickey Wray Wilson passes Thomas and leads by 29 miles ... Reed Finfrock is 27 miles behind Thomas ... Kaname Sakurai is 94 miles back.

Chapter Six

August 1, 1995

B etween Guymon, Oklahoma, and a lonely intersection called Slapout, population eight, my average speed was at best a paltry six or seven mph. That's about the pace of a grandmother out for a leisurely Sunday ride, and it was at least 10 mph slower than I wanted. The rolling fields of western Oklahoma seemed to drag on forever.

Slapout, the ceremonial midpoint of RAAM, is usually a welcome break from the monotony of the sage, wheat and cattle country of the Oklahoma panhandle. The community is perched on a small knoll and has only four buildings, three of them abandoned and decaying, making Slapout a modern-day snapshot of Steinbeck's *The Grapes of Wrath*. The lone active building is a Phillips 66 gas station at the junction of U.S. Highways 270 and 283. It's also a RAAM time station. Slapout, which literally rose from the dust bowl in 1932, doesn't receive much attention, except for those few summer days every year when RAAM pays a visit.

George and his father Norman wait for the rider change in Slapout during the 1993 Team RAAM.

The race has embraced Slapout, and the town has reciprocated, making it one of the few communities along the route that outwardly appreciates the events and riders. Ranchers and oilmen drive to the gas station in their dusty pickups and gather around a table in the store, where they talk about grain prices and nurse coffee while waiting for the next cyclist to arrive. The station owners, whose Cadillac sports license plates that read SLAPOUT, print RAAM T-shirts and have a white chalkboard that lets customers know which riders have passed through, and when.

I enjoyed my brief time there as a member of relay teams, but there would be no warm fuzzies this time. I was hurting and frustrated with the crew.

Bruce arrived after his sleep shift, saw my bedraggled looks and asked if I needed more food.

"No," I said, "it's my neck."

"Do you need more sleep?"

"No, it's my *neck*."

> *... nobody's listening to me! ... it's my neck!*
> *... I'm going so slow ... I can't hold up my head*
> *... nothing to look at here ... oh well, I can't see*
> *anything anyway ... wish I had something to*
> *take my mind off my neck ...*

The flat prairie was beginning to bend and serve up some steep rollers, requiring me to keep two hands on my bars. No longer could I use my hand to hold my head up. I could sense my chances of finishing within the 48-hour window slipping away. At least a steady rain was keeping me cool.

Fifty miles west of Slapout, I looked over my shoulder and could see Rickey Wray Wilson, the Texan who was entering familiar territory, gaining on me. Nothing is more exhilarating than passing a rider, and by the same token nothing is more demoralizing than getting passed. I already looked pretty ugly, with ice bags and Ace bandages on my knees, a TENS unit on my foot, dried blood on my fingers because of a broken shifting lever, and a dazed look on my face, but I refused to give Wilson any satisfaction. As he approached, I asked my crew for my electric razor, sat up in the saddle and began shaving while wearing a broad grin, as if I was just taking a short break and unconcerned about his passing.

He had no idea how much I was hurting. Worse, neither did my crew. Bruce was nonplussed and Bev was frightened. The others were helpless. I was deteriorating and nobody knew what to do. All they could do was sit in their vans and watch.

When we pulled into Slapout, I was still angry with Mike. I hadn't said anything to him about the aerobars as I labored across the rolling panhandle, but I did tersely tell him that I didn't want to see the titanium bicycle again. It might be lighter and faster, but if I couldn't lean on the aerobars it was useless.

> *... can't believe I snapped at Mike ... he's been such a loyal friend and supporter ... getting tired of the crew, but they're probably getting tired of me, too ...*

After Wilson disappeared on the horizon, I apologized to my crew for my surliness and went to bed in Slapout, whose population had doubled with the arrival of a dozen crew people who had no idea what to do next for their weakened rider.

The drives from Flagstaff to Oakland and from Oakland to Corvallis after my wicked seizures in May 1989 were the longest of my life. I was frightened. We stopped for two days in Oakland to visit Bev's aunt, then headed for home, where Bev immediately scheduled an appointment with my general practitioner, Dr. James Koski.

I underwent rigorous testing: Blood tests, CAT scans, an EEG with all the flashing lights. I was embarrassed because the doctors were trying to induce a seizure, and I'd never have one while under observation. I'd be frustrated and relieved at the same time—frustrated because I knew the doctors needed to see a seizure to know how to respond, but relieved because the episodes hurt and scared me. Invariably, on the way home from an appointment I'd have a seizure in the car with Bev.

I remember how angry and hurt I was to overhear Bev telling her friends I had epilepsy. I was still in denial. I also wondered what her parents thought of her new husband.

I finally had to face the truth in the words of my neurologist in Corvallis, Dr. Richard LaFrance, as much as I feared them: "You have epilepsy."

Epilepsy? I knew little about the disorder, except the stories about uncontrollable shaking and swallowed tongues. I was determined to learn more about an illness I'd probably had for five years.

We discovered that to function properly, the brain relies on millions of nerve cells communicating electrically. With epilepsy, some of these brain cells misfire. When this happens, a seizure ensues.

In simple terms, seizures are divided into two major groups, once called petit mal seizures and grand mal seizures

In what was formerly known as petit mal, partial or localized seizures begin in one portion of the brain. The victim may or may not lose consciousness, depending on what area of the brain is involved.

In what was once known as grand mal, the entire brain is affected and consciousness is altered. The victim initially stiffens ("tonic") and simultaneously loses consciousness, followed by rhythmic jerking called the "clonic" phase. This is the classic characterization of a grand mal seizure, now called "tonic-clonic." The result typically is exhaustion for hours, sometimes days.

I called the seizures "my demons." I always believed they were angry with me because I tried so hard to suppress them. Then when they finally escaped, they were violent and vindictive. The feeling of helplessness was immense. No amount of exercise or rehabilitation would eliminate the seizures. I lived every moment in fear of the next one, wondering when and where it would arrive, knowing for sure only that there would indeed be another one.

Where did the epilepsy come from? No one has been absolutely certain, but doctors speculate that it stemmed from the car accident in San Antonio. Tests eventually revealed small scars on my brain. The scars were either always there or, more likely, a result of the trauma to my brain. What precipitated the sudden violent seizures after five years of mild dizzy spells is anybody's guess. After telling my story to others with epilepsy, I've heard from many who went five or 10 years without a seizure and then—BOOM!—it hit them.

The diagnosis began a hellacious three months that made the rehab from the car accident seem like a walk in the park by comparison. The seizures were frightening enough, and getting worse, but there was more. My inability to take care of myself forced us to live with Bev's parents in Corvallis. My doctor was required to call the Department of Motor Vehicles, which in turn contacted me and ordered me to relinquish my driver's license. I was devastated. A driver's license is the primary form of societal identity. I didn't consider it a right to drive, but I also had a flawless driving record. I thought as an adult I deserved the dignity of making the wise decision to quit driving myself. The humiliation was further compounded when the DMV exchanged my driver's license for an ID card that noted my circumstances.

Early on, my summer on the slopes looked promising despite the seizures. I had started a ski school business with a partner. The number of signups excited us. My general practitioner, Dr. Koski, had referred me to Dr. LaFrance, who noted my active lifestyle and searched for a medication that he hoped would halt the episodes and limit side effects. At the time, about 16 drugs were available to arrest seizures. We settled on Tegretol, which has proven successful for thousands of epilepsy patients.

It failed miserably for me.

The seizures continued to increase in frequency and intensity, and now I had side effects from the medication. I honestly can't say which was worse—the seizures or the side effects. Without the medication, the seizures almost certainly would've been more violent, but the side effects made my life miserable beyond belief.

I tried to continue working as a ski instructor, but my balance was impaired and I was sensitive to light—two bad traits in a ski coach on a glacier where there's no shade. I tried wearing a big hat, but the light reflected off the snow, so even with sunscreen all over my face I was getting blister burns. I covered them with zinc oxide. For a while, I somehow managed to improve my skiing, which was good for my psyche, but then I started having more seizures.

One day I was standing in the kitchen, leaning over a big griddle on a stove, cooking sausage. I reached down to try one, got that minor dizzy feeling again and pitched forward. Fortunately the cabinets caught my head, knocking me backward and away from the skillet.

It was then that Bev and I were first introduced to public perceptions about epilepsy. Bev remained with me in the cabin that day and insisted that I sleep. I was sleeping when a skier's mother knocked on the door, peered inside and saw her child's instructor on the couch.

"What's going on?" she demanded.

"My husband had a seizure this morning," Bev replied patiently.

"Oh, we had a dog that had fits," the woman said. "That must be so frustrating."

Epilepsy isn't a glamorous disorder. It still carries a stigma. Until 1982, many states had laws prohibiting people with epilepsy to marry. Only 16 years earlier, President Lyndon B. Johnson repealed a law barring immigrants with the disorder to enter the country. In previous centuries, people were thought to be possessed by demons or to be mentally ill. They were often institutionalized.

The public has much more awareness today, but that doesn't make life any less frightening for those of us with epilepsy. We never know when it's going to strike next. In some ways, that's the worst part.

Walking down a sidewalk, I'd wonder where I was going to fall. I'd think about it everywhere I went. The fear wasn't about the seizure; it was about where I would land and how people would respond. I didn't want somebody calling an ambulance. I didn't want anybody thinking I could swallow my tongue, which is one of the great myths about epilepsy. The truth is, your jaw is clenched so tight it's impossible to swallow your tongue or anything else. During a seizure, my jaws and the remainder of my body were clenched for three to four minutes, which explains why I was so exhausted after seizures.

As the seizures continued, Dr. LaFrance kept increasing my dosage of Tegretol, eventually to the maximum allowed. I took three pills four times a day. After a few hours, when the medicine began to wear off, I'd feel better, but then it was time to take the next dose. It was the first thing I did every morning and the last thing I did before bed every night.

Tegretol works well for many people, but not for me. This is one of the frustrations people with epilepsy must deal with—that a treatment will help one patient and not the next. There's no way to predict.

I grew weaker by the day. I couldn't venture into sunlight because my eyes hurt. Television also was painful. I couldn't read words because they raced around on the page, a side effect of the medication. I had to quit riding a bicycle, stop running and ultimately could barely walk. I was forced to quit my job as a ski instructor. Eventually, I was so weak that I was reduced to lapping broth out of a soup bowl on the floor because tremors made my hands shake so much I couldn't hold a spoon. Later I'd have to wear mini-pads because I couldn't completely control my bladder.

I began to feel as if it was my fault the medication wasn't working. Truthfully, I wasn't sure it *wasn't* working. If I weren't on Tegretol, I might've been having multiple seizures daily. In my misery, I'd think that perhaps I should feel grateful.

Compounding my esteem problem were my visits to the doctor. I was always intimidated. Doctors had an aura of superiority. When your self-confidence is shot and you're with a person of such high regard, you're assuming he's making all the best decisions for you. So when he'd ask about my side effects and seizure activity, I wouldn't go into much detail. I'd tell him I was fine. He'd run me through a battery of tests where I'd be lying down, wires hooked to my head and different patterns of light flashing before me. They wanted to produce a seizure to see what portion of the brain was causing the episodes, but I'd fight it the entire time because I didn't want to go through it. Then, in the car on the way home, I'd have a seizure while Bev was driving.

Three months after that first major seizure in Flagstaff, there was no end in sight. I was surrounded by dozens of well-meaning people, all looking for answers while wringing their hands in increasing futility and despair. I realized amid my fog that I might have to be on this drug for the remainder of my life, however short that might be. I wondered about my quality of life. I began to think the only relief would be death. There were times I considered it a viable option.

One day, Bev was driving me to the hospital for a doctor's appointment when I saw the telltale little black spot out of the corner of my eye, blanking out my vision. I knew a particularly nasty seizure loomed. I had forgotten that Bev had fed me dozens of green grapes several hours earlier. I tilted the passenger seat all the way back and braced for the eruption.

I was powerless to prevent it, too weak to fight it and too debilitated even to move. The seizure lasted about five minutes. When I came to I projectile-vomited, splattering the grapes off the roof of the car and watching helplessly while they returned to my mouth, filling my air passages. I couldn't turn my head, so I laid there immobilized, drowning in my own vomit. At first, I had a sense of abject terror, then I began to think absurd thoughts, which I later learned is typical for people who are close to drowning. My brain reached a point where it was telling me it was okay to breathe, and I suddenly let go of all my fears.

"I'm going to die like a rock star!" I remember thinking to myself.

Bev responded quickly and saved my life. She stopped the car and turned my head, clearing my mouth and throat, allowing me to breathe freely again. Then she turned the car around and drove home, where she cut me out of my clothes. Then she called the doctor and said we needed an immediate appointment that afternoon. It was then that Dr. LaFrance, to his everlasting credit, finally admitted that he and my existing treatment were no match for my epilepsy. He had done some research and learned of an experimental program at the Oregon Health Sciences University some 90 miles north up Interstate 5 in Portland.

The investigational drug, not yet approved by the Food and Drug Administration, was called Lamictal. A pharmaceutical company called GlaxoWellcome, now GlaxoSmithKline, produced it. Dr. Mark Yerby, one of the nation's foremost epilepsy experts, headed the program.

Lamictal was the miracle I needed.

The drug immediately controlled my seizures. The next major step was finding the proper dosage to minimize or hopefully eliminate the side effects. That would take time.

My depth perception was gone and I struggled with balance. I'd sit in a chair and feel as if I were levitating toward the ceiling. Sometimes I'd feel as if I were sitting above a table full of people, looking down on them. I'd wrap my arms around the armrest and my feet around the legs because then I'd feel the chair tip forward. It was bizarre.

Another side effect was quintuple vision. I always saw five Bevs. When she drove me around I'd see five roads and five oncoming cars. On two-lane roads the cars always looked as if they were coming right at us. I'd have to hide my eyes. I could never tell which car was real and which four weren't.

Incredibly, many people cracked inane jokes like, "Wow, man, I'd have to spend a lot of money to get drugs that would do that for me!" I can't fathom why anybody would want to have an experience like that.

As I slowly improved, I began to yearn for exercise. My lack of depth perception eliminated bicycling, but I learned I could run safely by wearing a white glove and holding it in front of me as a guide. I could sense where my arm was, so I could run if had my hand in sight. My body awareness would take over and I'd know where to put my feet.

By November, I decided it was time to return to work. I pursued a part-time position as skiing coach for Crescent Valley High School in Corvallis. I was forthright about my disorder. I showed them my resume and then said, "Here's what I've got, but I also have epilepsy." Many friends advised against me revealing my illness, but it was important for me to be honest. Crescent Valley hired me. I didn't drive the team; I rode the bus or joined my students' parents. And I skied with the team in practice. How? The same way I ran: With my hand out in front of me.

In February 1990, nine months after Flagstaff, the State of Oregon reissued my driver's license. I had met the criteria for being seizure-free, which is six months. It was a great feeling going back to the DMV.

When my vision cleared enough, my dad offered me a job with him in the insurance business in San Antonio. Fortunately, though only eight hospitals in the country had the clinical trial in which I was participating, Portland and San Antonio each had one. Bev and I moved to Texas and rented an apartment. Because light still bothered my eyes, I had to wear big, dark sunglasses everywhere. People stared, but I learned to ignore them.

I wasn't cured of epilepsy, and there were no guarantees I would be seizure-free the remainder of my life, but now I had a treatment that would allow me to live a normal life again.

There were many memorable dates that year, but none more important than August 28, 1989. On that day, three months and yet a lifetime after Flagstaff, I had a routine seizure.

It was my last one.

When I awoke from my nap in Slapout, I stepped out of the motor home and could scarcely believe my eyes.

While I was sleeping, Mike had rebuilt the entire front end of the titanium bicycle. He widened the aerobars, which took the pressure off my back muscles and gave me a more comfortable ride. He added a high-rise stem that enabled me to sit more upright. My faith in Mike would never waver again.

In the motor home, Bruce had been giving me a pep talk, telling me I was doing fine but that I had to increase my average speed. I glared at him and told him nobody wanted to go faster than I did, but that it wouldn't happen until we fixed my neck. At first I was irate at Bruce, particularly when the camera crew approached to see me in my trashed condition. I couldn't hold my head up, my knees pulsated and I was feeling sorry for myself, and there was Bruce telling me to go faster.

> *... when you're going eight mph you don't need anyone telling you you're slow! ... just fix my neck! ...*

I realized he was right, of course. I was in a race. I had to get over it. When I saw my new bike, I was instantly over it. I was excited. I could place my right hand on my forehead to keep my head tilted up yet still lay on the aerobars. I felt again that I would be okay, that I would make it to Savannah.

After a few miles, I summoned my crew and, as they rolled alongside in the van, told them how great I felt and that my ride would be perfect if I had something on which to rest my chin.

"I'm already on it," Mike reported cheerfully.

Ninety miles later, as the Plains began to give way to the more lush and humid country near Woodward, Oklahoma, we pulled over and Mike pulled out an Evian water bottle. He duct-taped it upside-down on the stem of my handlebars, giving me a place to rest my chin. The handling of the bicycle became more sensitive because my weight was forward, and the chin rest was so comfortable that drifting off to sleep was a very real concern. My neck problem wasn't cured, either, but now I wouldn't need a hand to keep my head up. I was much more aerodynamically sound.

At Woodward, the day crew gave way to Bev's night crew, which had secretly gotten calzones and fettuccine alfredo at a restaurant. I felt guilty eating it because the day crew was working so diligently to keep me on a strict program. I struggled because I felt loyalty to both crews.

That night, as I pushed toward Arkansas, the skies opened up with a classic downpour. My chin slid on the bottom of the Evian bottle, and I began to bleed as the seam and little plastic point irritated my skin. We stopped at a gas station for a break to put a pad on the water bottle. Reed Finfrock was there, looking miserable. It was hard to see other people looking so bad, but I also realized I wasn't the only one hurting.

The rebuilt bike and water bottle provided instant hope but weren't a cure-all. The side effects would persist, at least for a while. My neck still hurt, my chin burned and my muscles ached. The rain was so relentless it knocked out one of the loudspeakers, preventing my crew from playing music. It also caused the TENS unit to give me painful electrical shocks.

> *... my chin's going to look real pretty at the end ... Reed looks so sleepy and physically spent ... at least I'm passing somebody ...*

Just outside of Kingfisher, Oklahoma, we called it a day and I met with both crews before I went down for my nightly break. I looked horrible again. I had ice bags and Ace bandages on both knees and the TENS unit on my Achilles. Death warmed over would've been a kind description.

I had begun to hallucinate again and act irrationally. At one point I ordered Eric to remove the water bottle serving as chin rest.

"Why?" he asked. "Isn't it comfortable?"

"Yes," I said.

"Then why do you want to take it off?"

I couldn't say.

"I know I'm not going very fast," I said, "but I've got to make up time and I think the best way to make up time is to cut back on sleep breaks. I have to keep moving. Even if it's in single digits, I'm still moving. We really need to come together and ride for as long as we can with no sleep."

The crew wasn't so certain, but I'd been in this position before, six years earlier, with my seizures. We'd found ways to mask the pain in my Achilles and knees, and now, after reaching my ebb hours earlier, the chin rest had become a mask for the most debilitating part of all—my neck.

Eventually, I was confident, when I reached my inevitable equilibrium down the road, I'd be fine.

I stripped naked and, dazed, crashed in the back of the van, hoping that a fitful rest would give me the energy boost needed to cut back on later sleep breaks.

August 2, 1995
Woodward, Oklahoma

Rob Kish has reached Time Station 40 in Lonoke, Arkansas, 392 miles ahead of George Thomas and 42 ahead of Danny Chew ... Seana Hogan and Muffy Ritz are still third and fourth, followed by Dieter Weik (123 miles behind), Gerry Tatrai (165), Beat Gfeller (230), Tom Davies (250), Bruno Heer (270) and Thomas, who is one mile ahead of Rickey Wray Wilson and 28 in front of Reed Finfrock ... Paul Solon has dropped out because of a viral problem.

Chapter Seven

August 2, 1995

I awoke outside of Kingfisher on the morning of what promised to be a hot but bearable day. I was so determined to cover the final 1,000 miles with limited sleep breaks that I tried relieving myself while riding. Being a bit shy, I waited until the road cleared, but my attempt to accomplish what so many others in RAAM routinely do proved futile.

For a time, the race was even fun again—mostly because it was a race again. Mike read the hysterical *Weekly World News* over the speakers, making me chuckle. He was reading something about Albert Einstein's brain in storage as we drove by a cemetery in Shawnee, Oklahoma, where a funeral was in progress. At another point, we rolled past a golf course, and over the loudspeakers Eric announced, "All the way from Los Angeles, California … George THOMAS!"

I had been so worried about my neck that I had forgotten about the race. Now my crew was telling me I was about 36 hours behind the leader, giving me a cushion. I wasn't pedaling briskly, but at least I was pedaling. Some-where in central Oklahoma I passed Rickey Wray Wilson, who apparently had been sleeping. I suddenly went from behind him to ahead of him without knowing it.

At Shawnee, just east of Oklahoma City, my crew de-cided that I was foolish to avoid sleep and ordered me to take a brief break. To them, I looked awful. My feet had ballooned from my normal size 10 to size 12. Fortunately, like Shermer Neck, I had read about this malady in RAAM and brought larger shoes for the latter part of the race.

While I was snoozing, the Kern Wheelmen relay team passed me. The relay teams start two days after the soloists in RAAM and always catch them. The Kern Wheelmen from California were the first to catch me. I missed them, but soon after I began riding again. Team Brazil ap-proached, with two cars ahead of their racer. They honked and cheered as they drove past, giving me a shot of adrena-line. My old teammates from PacifiCare were in third and I was eager to see them. The heavens opened up again and we began to hit the short but steep climbs of the Ozark foothills in southeastern Oklahoma.

> *… relay teams are already catching me?*
> *… I didn't want to get caught until Arkansas*
> *or Tennessee … I'm only in Oklahoma … it's*
> *just another way of being told I'm slow …*

We stopped at a convenience store to tend to my saddle sores. An extra pad I was using on top of the bandages was stuck to my skin, and as Bev and Sabra tried to remove it gently, they dropped it on the filthy bathroom floor. It was my last pad. The three of us stood, staring at the slimy mess, before Sabra reached down, peeled it off the tiles and washed it in the sink. She remedicated it and rebandaged the sores, which to my amazement were heal-ing, and then I returned to the pouring rain.

I wasn't the only one who looked awful. Eric said he was tripping over the bags under his eyes. In the rain, my food was soaked, ruining the one aspect of RAAM I truly enjoyed—eating. Even sleep wasn't blissful. After 21 hours on a bike, I always felt like I'd just stepped off a rocking boat or treadmill.

As we pushed toward Arkansas, the rain subsided. I was so sleepy I reluctantly asked for the chocolate-covered coffee beans. Bev warned me against it, but gave in. I should've listened. I crossed into Arkansas with an upset, bloated stomach, then begged to use the motor home restroom manned by a race official at the next time station. We tossed the coffee beans in the garbage.

Steam rose from the road as I pedaled steadily into the hill country. Eventually I noticed a van ahead. I was catching a rider. It was Reed Finfrock, in his telltale pink helmet and Lycra. I joined Reed and we rode together briefly, sharing our tales of agony and ecstasy. I could see that he was enjoying it as much as I was. We had developed a competitive bond since Arizona, staging a race within a race for eighth place. The passing and repassing was stressful, and I was definitely racing against him, but I also wanted Reed to finish and get his ring. We were kindred spirits.

After what seemed like moments, my crew ordered us to separate. RAAM rules prohibit riders pedaling together for longer than 15 minutes. The idea is for soloists to complete the race on their own, without the camaraderie of fellow riders. We reluctantly said good-bye and I pedaled off.

I was taking a brief bathroom break by the side of the road when I saw the first PacifiCare van. I eagerly jumped on my bike, expecting my acquaintances to cheer or wave. They barely acknowledged me. We leapfrogged briefly; rider Steve Horn said hello and asked how I was doing as he passed, and then he was gone. That was it. Nobody in PacifiCare's pace van said a word. I saw their shuttle van one last time and heard somebody cheer, but by that point I was secretly rooting for Team Brazil to hold them off.

The response from my old friends disappointed me, but the good news was I was getting past some of my physical ailments. When I awoke from my afternoon nap in Shawnee, Sabra said I was a new man. I quit being picky about ice and quit quibbling about where to put the TENS unit. She said I completely changed, from a pain standpoint, as if I had said to myself, "Okay, it's here, just deal with it."

> *… just wanna get on my bike and ride …*
> *seeing more riders and crews helps … sorry the*
> *Brazilians are gone already … they're fun …*
> *relay teams go by soooo fast …*

I was finally learning to live with the pain. Now I could focus on getting faster and moving on with my race. I actually began to pick up my pace. I limited my stops. At one point race official Chris Kostman went past holding out a hand with his RAAM ring on it as if it were a carrot. In 1987, at the age of 20, Kostman became, and remains, the youngest person to finish RAAM officially.

"George, you've got to quit coasting so much," he exhorted. "Keep pedaling."

The decision to start treatments with Lamictal wasn't cut and dried.

The drug wasn't approved by the FDA until 1994. It had been available and quite successful for five years in Europe, where anti-seizure clinical trials often use a standard drug against the investigational compound. But the

FDA won't accept the data from such studies even when results indicate *equivalence* in two drugs. The FDA contends that while results may indicate equivalence, it might mean that neither drug was effective in the study population or other groups.

To satisfy FDA requirements, a study drug must prove *superior* in one part of a clinical trial next to another drug. Only then can it be marketed in the United States.

I was scared. As a red, white and true blue Texan, who was I to question the FDA's reasoning? If it wasn't good enough yet for my government, I wasn't sure it was good enough for me. Even scarier than the uncertainty of an unproven drug was the realization that I would participate in a so-called "double blind" test. Some participants would get Lamictal, some a placebo. I knew I didn't want a placebo.

At least I was finally beginning to wrestle control of my life away from the epilepsy and its side effects. I also trusted Dr. Yerby. Though it might sound corny, I thought the experiment was worthy because even if it didn't work for me, Lamictal might help someone else with epilepsy.

Lamictal had instantly rendered me seizure-free, but I was still fearful about the lingering physical and emotional scars of epilepsy. As my friend Dr. Steven Schachter, a renowned epileptologist from Harvard Medical School, likes to say, "Seizures are now and then, but the side effects are always there."

To ensure the proper attention during my recovery, Bev and I had moved to San Antonio, where I could work for my father. Racing never entered my mind. I was afraid of the road. The chaos of a big city made it easy to justify not riding my bicycle through town. San Antonio couldn't have been a more bike-unfriendly city. It had no bike lanes. Eventually I tried to drive, but when my doctor in San Antonio found out, he was angry. He threatened to have my license taken away. He was concerned about the side effects. So for two years, my dad drove me to work every morning, and I ran home every night.

Finally, in 1991, my disdain for dependence eventually motivated me to buy a mountain bike and start commuting. It was fun getting out on a bike again, and eventually I pulled my old road bike out, dusted off the cobwebs, jumped on and went for my first ride in two years. Every ride reinvigorated me just a little more. I acquired clipless pedals and new shoes. The more equipment I bought, the more excited I got.

Riding again gave me a sense of freedom I hadn't known in years. I could get away from the city on my own and find scenic places to ride. Once I got comfortable on the bike again, I started riding with Will Rotzler, the person who got me into racing after my accident in 1984. We're still good friends. I admired Will and his incredible leg muscles. I thought of him as some kind of cycling god.

George and PacifiCare teammate Steve Horn ride together briefly as Steve begins his leg of the 1993 Team RAAM.

Cycling has the image of an arrogant, elitist sport. Will embraced a geeky newcomer and was always encouraging. When I was slow, he'd slow down and ride with me. He had nothing to prove. He just wanted me to feel welcome.

Will put on a Tuesday night series and asked me to be the announcer. He knew if I was out there I'd want to ride. On my first try, I pedaled 10 laps and dropped out, but each week I improved. I enjoyed riding in a group and competing again, and my gains motivated me. I started riding every day. I was in the citizen's category, where anybody could ride, but no matter. For the first time since my seizures three years earlier, I could continually measure my improvement.

One weekend in 1992, I entered a stage race featuring a time trial, criterium and road race. I won all three. Soon after, I was reinstated in the USCF's Category 3, where I had been before the seizures. They said it was clear I had no need to work my way back up.

This was all within three months of first getting on a bike again.

One day the president of PacifiCare in Texas was in my dad's office and saw a photo of me riding.

"I didn't know you race bikes," he said to me, adding, "I've been wanting to put some money in a team."

Cycling became that much more important. Will and I put together Team PacifiCare, a masters team. We now talked optimistically about securing more sponsorships. We were a strong team with solid results every week.

How to explain my quick success at bicycle racing after so many years of inactivity? I can't say.

My percentage of body fat isn't extraordinary. I'm not terribly strong. My VO_2max is ordinary. One possible answer came in the late 1990s, when I joined a group of cyclists at Oregon State University for testing designed to show how ultra-marathoners are different from typical weekend warriors. An OSU graduate student was studying whether endorphins affect heart rate. Some of us were injected with a placebo and others with endorphin blockers. A doctor watching the test was surprised to see my heart rate quickly jump to 110, then go no higher, regardless of how hard I worked. He told me I had the perfect makeup for my sport. It enabled me to keep a sustained pace amid challenging conditions. There was a time when I'd get frustrated during training rides because I'd work my legs to the max and still my heart rate was low. I finally accepted that I was just different and built for ultra-marathon cycling.

The upshot is that an ordinary man is capable of achieving extraordinary feats. I was getting excited about a career in racing and having fun in sports. I was eager to train.

Still, I had more important things to think about. By then, Meredith, who was born in 1991, was two years old. I had a full-time job and I had returned to school for some postgraduate courses. I wanted to race, but finding the time to train properly was challenging. I squeezed in as many night rides as I could.

The best part of being seizure-free was being able to swim with Meredith and take her on drives without fear of mishaps. I appreciated the mundane daily tasks that most of us take for granted.

Now, though, instead of people expressing amazement that I was cycling so soon after an accident, it was, "Wow, you have seizures and look what you've overcome!"

I pedaled into Fort Smith, Arkansas, at about 1 a.m. for my nap and a crew change. My mom made me some delicious barley soup. Our schedule didn't even remotely resemble the plan. Crew changes had drifted from the expected 9 a.m. and 9 p.m. shifts to 9 a.m. and 1 a.m. Bruce stuck rigidly to his schedule, but Bev's crew arrived later and later each night. Bruce's crew wasn't getting any sleep.

The animosity between the two crews was building to an explosive head. A fight seemed inevitable. I didn't know what the squabbling was about, but I had sensed it all along. The tension created a stress that I didn't need. I liked each member of the crew individually, so it was difficult to grasp why they were so upset with each other. When Bruce was in charge during the day, I liked him and was confident in his command. When Bev was on at night, I was confident then, too. Their attitudes and approaches were dramatically different. The night crew was much less structured. They tried to keep the ambience light and fun, believing that would help keep me awake. When Bruce was on, it was all business.

Later I learned they were arguing about how best to take care of me again. They all knew about my determination to finish within 48 hours of the winner, and they knew I was teetering on the brink. Everyone had different ideas about how to accomplish it without burying me. Race official Chris Kostman told me I should use my sleep breaks for just that—sleep. No massages, no showers, no food, no strategy sessions. Bev agreed, but Bruce always spent 30 minutes talking about strategy. Bruce also wanted to get more proteins into me to build my muscles. Bev argued that my muscles were shriveling because I wasn't getting enough carbohydrates.

"This race—and I use the term loosely—is just a matter of who can tolerate the most pain and abuse, at a higher rate of speed, i.e., 17 mph over 3,000 miles instead of 14," Bev wrote in her RAAM journal. "It's insane."

About the only thing they all agreed on was that each shift needed to get about 160 miles out of me over 12 hours to have a chance.

I tried to ignore them. At one point in Arkansas, the van had a flat tire and had to stop. I barely noticed. Suddenly I was riding alone. I enjoyed serenity reminiscent of my youth in Texas and all those solo journeys in Oregon. The sunrise just past Fort Smith was gorgeous, and I reveled again in surprising newfound strength. Though I didn't know it at the time, more than two-thirds of the field had dropped out, and several other riders were more than a full day behind me. I was focusing solely on closing the gap on the riders in front of me.

My crew pulled alongside, told me they needed to get the tire repaired, pointed me in the right direction and told me I'd be fine until they returned.

> *... all right, everything on my body's fixed ... it's hot, humid ... wish the rain would come back ... can I still make 48 hours? ... don't think about the crew ... it's their problem ... gotta make 48 hours ... I think I can make it ... I really can ...*

For the first time, despite all my aches and pains and crew tensions, I was actually beginning to believe it.

August 3-4, 1995
Mississippi River

Hurricane Erin is slowing the leaders, ending Rob Kish's dream of breaking his RAAM record of eight days, three hours and 11 minutes set in 1992. He crosses the Georgia state line and is expected to arrive in Savannah at 8 a.m. Aug. 5 with a time of eight days and 20 hours ... Danny Chew is three hours behind Kish, Seana Hogan is five and Muffy Ritz is seven ... George Thomas is 11th, sandwiched between Reed Finfrock and Rickey Wray Wilson ... The Kern Wheelmen, averaging 21 mph, have passed most of the soloists and are expected to catch Kish and Chew just before the finish.

Chapter Eight

August 3-4, 1995

The dog days of RAAM. Most of the challenging terrain was behind me, but I was still distant enough from the finish—nearly 800 miles—that the ordeal seemed far from over. I was laboring on flat terrain in surprisingly moderate, calm and sunny weather.

My crew solved some of my nutritional problems by making me fruit kabobs. They'd hand me strawberries, bananas, watermelon, cantaloupe and sometimes a Power Bar on a stick. I could eat and stay on my aerobars. Meanwhile, unbeknownst to me, Reed passed me again while I took a brief sleep break in Dardanelle, Arkansas, about 70 miles northwest of Little Rock.

Bruce was angry at the night crew for swimming at the motel pool while I slept. He said they weren't focused on the race, that they should be sleeping or doing something race-oriented. He was also angry that the night crew was late—again—for a shift change.

He was anxious about my pace.

"We need more discipline during rest stops to make them more efficient if we're going to make it," he said. "But we can't even get the other crew to meet us on time for the shift change."

Bev replied, "I know that Bruce wants us to stay on schedule, but we want to spend some time following George during the day. So we've been pushing the shift change back a little each day."

The tension between the crews was building toward an explosion that I was helpless to prevent. I tried to ignore the crew spats and focus on my riding.

After my nap, I got back on my bike with renewed zeal to catch Reed. I pedaled briskly through Conway, Arkansas, and felt reasonably strong as dusk descended.

That night, a coed relay team called the Azio Saddle Tramps came racing by with Reed pacing them, which was legal. He looked awesome. Somewhere I must have passed him while he was napping. The last time I saw him he looked awful.

"Hey George!" Reed yelled cheerfully. "We're going to make it!"

… yeah, well, maybe you will …

My left knee was the size of a grapefruit. My right Achilles had swollen to the point where there was no definition between my knee and my swollen foot. My fingers were numb and bloodied from the broken shifter.

I was accustomed to pain and had simply come to accept it, but I worried about my body. All I could think about was finishing within the 48-hour mark. To come this far, hurt this badly and expend this much effort without earning a ring would be devastating. My mind was strong, but my body was struggling to meet the challenge.

Somewhere in the Arkansas night, a guy yelled out, "Hey, a girl went by here two days ago—you suck!" I wanted to offer a snappy retort, but all I could say was, "Yeah, I do." I was frustrated by my inability to push myself in good weather conditions. I should have been making up time. In the darkness, I couldn't read the speed on my computer, but I felt slow and had no energy. I was sure my speed was in single digits.

Sleepiness began to overtake me as I reached another low point on par with the desert of California, the east flank of Wolf Creek Pass and the panhandle of Oklahoma. I stared at the side of U.S. Highway 64 in central Arkansas, thinking how the shoulder looked as soft as a mattress. All I wanted was to lie down there and drift off to sleep. The urge to pull over and sleep on the pavement was unbelievable. My crew gave me a Coca-Cola and piece of chocolate, and the sugar rush regenerated me for about a half-hour, but then I grew even sleepier. In its own way, this had become the most challenging part of the race.

> *... asphalt looks so soft, warm and inviting ... never been this sleepy ... ever ... just wanna lie down on the road ... gonna pull over, drop my bike and lay down ... you guys aren't going to make me move ...*

I went down for a nap in Forest City, Arkansas, and thought about crossing the Mississippi, where RAAM legend Pete Penseyres says the race truly begins. Until then, the riders see it as a 2,200-mile parade start—an agonizing, painful, exhausting, sleep-deprived 2,200-mile parade start.

After all that, I was losing hope.

The reality of RAAM's immense challenge began to sink in about nine months before the race.

Until then I had sensed only a romanticism associated with ultra-marathon cycling—the pedaling through the night, the beautiful scenery, the adventure. My racing friends ridiculed endurance cycling and its participants, but I was strangely drawn to it. For years I'd said RAAM was a race I wanted to do.

I just never imagined that I could go through with it.

After suffering my seizures and the subsequent side effects, though, I needed something to prove myself whole again. Ski instructing had started well, but I was forced to quit. I never felt good about returning to San Antonio to work with my dad, even though it was a plush job financially and otherwise. If we had stayed, I'm sure I'd be living in a nice house in the San Antonio suburbs and driving nice cars.

George and team PacifiCare finish in first place in Savannah, Georgia in 1993.

To help prepare for the 1995 RAAM, George participated in the three-week PAC Tour from San Diego to Charleston, S.C. Here he is riding in Arizona with Muffy Ritz.

The accident and epilepsy left me wanting more personal fulfillment. Marathon bicycle racing offered that. I could never win the Tour de France or the Hawaii Ironman Triathlon, and I had no interest in climbing Mount Everest or kayaking the Colorado River. But I needed some avenue to prove myself. Bicycle racing was the natural answer.

After earning my USCF Category 3 rating again in San Antonio, I began to ride in masters races. My friend Steve Horn and I recruited Team PacifiCare with the express purpose of competing in the world's toughest bicycle race.

Team PacifiCare won Team RAAM in 1993, and although I struggled in the desert I grew stronger as the race progressed. Trouble was, I entered with the wrong attitude. I looked at participants in Team RAAM, including me, as cyclists who couldn't do it solo. I imagined winning Team RAAM was a great achievement, but there was no thrill at all. It was compounded by the arrogance of my teammates, who acted as if it was a monumental achievement when they passed solo riders. I thought to myself that I'd almost rather finish last in the solo race than win Team RAAM.

Nevertheless, I returned with the same team in the summer of 1994, again with an inappropriate attitude. I didn't want to be there at all. I wanted to be there solo. My teammates seemed even more insufferable. They printed T-shirts saying, "Losing is not an option." I found myself secretly cheering when other teams passed us. Every time one did, I'd think, "Second is not an option" or "Third is not an option," and so on. We finished fifth.

Before even considering a solo effort in RAAM, I wanted to get a sense of riding across the country, so I joined RAAM cofounder Lon Haldemann on one of his annual PAC Tour rides. I was waffling on whether to enter the Furnace Creek 508 as a RAAM qualifier, and I thought the three-week PAC Tour ride from San Diego to Charleston, South Carolina, would be a stern test. I was in mediocre condition at the beginning and it was a struggle, but I gradually improved as we pedaled approximately 120 miles daily. Still, I had no delusions of grandeur—120 miles is less than half the mileage needed daily to successfully navigate RAAM.

Nevertheless, in October 1994, I entered the Furnace Creek 508, which goes from Valencia to Twenty-Nine Palms, California, and includes 35,000 feet of climbing. It has one of the highest dropout rates of any ultra-marathon bicycle race.

As I stood with my bicycle at the starting line, I shivered while contemplating the daunting task ahead. This nonstop ride would be far more challenging than Team RAAM. I had never raced solo longer than 166 miles. My identifier was "Timber Wolf." I enlisted a crew of two and we decorated the van accordingly.

I was strong early and kept my planned pace. The only struggle was with my ego. I was far back of the leaders and tempted to chase. But I always managed to keep the big picture in mind. It was better to pass than be passed. After 180 miles, my knees were sore, so I washed down a Naprocin with a Coke. One of my crew members, Dave Marshall, gave me a rubdown and got me rolling again. I was 13th, two hours behind the leaders.

I began to play leapfrog in the darkness with "Mule" and then began the signature midrace 13-mile climb on a nine percent grade. When I reached the top, now in 12th place, the pass looked like a hospital ward. Lights and bodies were everywhere. Nearly everyone who was ahead of me had stopped for a rest at the summit.

Dave's brother, Larry, gave me a warm set of clothes for the dark descent, and I sped downhill at better than 50 mph. My bicycle was out-handling the van on the corners, so I was in almost total darkness, save for the small beacon on my handlebars. By now I'd passed seven riders. In two hours, I'd climbed from 13th to sixth.

The night would become a blur of rigorous climbs and freezing descents. Kaname Sakurai, aka "Sea Lion," passed me at a rapid pace, but I caught him when he took a break. The scenario would continue through the night. I passed another van with the name "Wolverine" etched on the hood. It was Dieter Weik, who was on the Kern Wheelmen team that defeated us earlier in the summer in Team RAAM. I'd also heard he would be attempting his first solo RAAM in 1995.

Now I was in fifth, and I could see the lights of Baker, California, in the distance as a slight glow crept into the eastern sky.

With one eye over my shoulder, I pedaled at 20 mph and continued to play leapfrog with Sea Lion. After a 20-mile descent into Amboy, with 40 miles remaining, I learned from my crew that I was five minutes out of third. I was in dire need of a bathroom stop, but I pressed on, motivated by the sight of the van following "Duck" ahead. I doubted I could maintain my pace with a long, hot climb over the Sheep Hole Mountains ahead, but I downed a Snickers bar and a warm Coke and reached the summit with no one in sight on either side.

I arrived in Twenty-Nine Palms in third place, 12 minutes out of second. My surprising finish instantly had me contemplating RAAM. I had qualified, yes, but now going the distance seemed within my grasp.

Not long after my finish, my stomach became intensely nauseated, forcing me to sit. Once down, my knees locked and I couldn't rise. My father, Dave and Larry helped me to my motel room, where I showered and immediately collapsed into bed.

As I lay there, marveling at how sore and tired I felt, but thrilled that I was third, I was sobered by the realization that if I were in RAAM, I'd merely be in Flagstaff, with 2,400 miles still to go. I'd have to climb on my bike in a few hours and pedal a version of Furnace Creek all over again, and repeat the exercise for at least a week with less than four hours of sleep per night.

RAAM's romanticism vanished as its stark realities reared their ominous psychological heads, one after another. I wasn't sure if I could do it.

But I still wanted to try.

After the sleep break in Forrest City, I got a brief second wind and was riding at 20-plus mph as I headed toward West Memphis, Arkansas, and the Mississippi River as the sun rose.

My crew acquired another McDonald's bacon, egg and cheese biscuit for breakfast. I noticed at the time station in West Memphis that race leader Rob Kish of Port Orange, Florida, had passed through Calhoun, Georgia, 350 miles from the finish. I still had 800 to go. I pondered my chances as I shaved in the car while we drove over the Mississippi, which is required by RAAM rules.

> *Only two more states to go ... Tennessee is long ... and hilly ... don't know if I can make it in time ... how nice it would be to be in Georgia right now ...*

The weather had been almost perfect through Arkansas, but it was the proverbial calm before the storm. Just before West Memphis, I'd turned a corner in the darkness of my eighth night of RAAM and pedaled straight into the remnants of Hurricane Erin. The rains were torrential and the winds were constant.

When I reached Memphis, Tennessee after dawn, I was buffeted by the storm's powerful headwinds. Discouragement returned. Deep down I knew everybody else was tired and hurting, but I was at least 40 hours behind the leader. I was certain the cyclists ahead of me had passed through western Tennessee ahead of the storm.

> *This is going to kill me ... Kish was through here two days ago and probably missed all this ... no way I can make it in time ... no way ...*

After all I had overcome, I really thought I was finished again. I was depressed. This was my lowest emotional point yet. I stopped east of Memphis and dismounted. I was convinced there was no way I'd finish officially. All the effort and pain was for naught. Bev got out, came up to me and gave me a big hug.

"I'm proud of you," she said.

Moments later, Mike and Cindy Rourke, two race officials with whom I became close friends as the race progressed, arrived and told me how much they enjoyed having me in the event. They said they appreciated my demeanor. They also gave me the news that I was projected to finish 43 hours behind Kish. Rejuvenated emotionally if not physically, I reboarded my bike and pedaled strongly throughout the day.

As had been the case throughout RAAM, just as it seemed as if I could no go farther, I coaxed a fire in my belly that I didn't know existed. It came out of nowhere, and I can't explain it. I felt great. I picked up speed despite Erin's strong winds. I enjoyed the rural scenery of southwest Tennessee.

My renewed vigor was tempered when Bev pulled alongside with the night crew and told me that Bruce had ordered her and Eric off the crew. Bruce had become even more upset that the night crew was consistently late for shift changes, costing him three hours of vital sleep. The night crew still wanted some time to follow me in the day. East of Memphis, Bruce had warned Bev that if the night crew was late one more time, he would take Sabra into his van and send Bev and Eric home.

> *... I'm tired ... why does this keep happening? ... I don't need this ... this should NOT be my problem ... Bev gives me a huge emotional lift, and now she's not going to be on the*

*crew? ... Bruce can't just send somebody home
... especially Bev ... can't believe this ...*

This was yet another defining moment for me in RAAM. At first, I tried to solve their problems for them. Mike kept telling me not to worry about it, to just keep riding. Finally I decided I'd had it with all of them. They were upset because they're not sleeping? Give me a break. At that point, I knew I had to disconnect from the crew or the discord would eat me up.

After that, I just focused on riding. The towns and checkpoints—Bolivar, Lawrenceburg, Pulaski, Fayetteville—seemed to zip past on U.S. Highway 64. I was forced off the road by a semi truck, but I forged ahead despite jangled nerves. Even the rain was bearable because it was so warm.

I saw the motor home in the parking lot of a gas station ahead and groaned. I wanted to ride the crest of my energy. I wanted no more stops the rest of the way. Reluctantly, I gave in to my crew and took my two-hour afternoon sleep break.

I woke up feeling fine, but nowhere near as strong as I had been. My foot slipped off my pedal as I tried to mount the bicycle, causing me to drop several inches onto my saddle. Ouch! At least I still had feeling down there.

The heavy rains came in fits and starts, forcing me to stop regularly to don rain gear or take it off. Though the temperatures were warm, I shivered in the rain without my jacket. When the rain stopped, the jacket was suffocating. At one stop after dusk, I put my metal cleat onto the pavement and slipped, careening to the asphalt. The film crew turned this minor slip into one of the most dramatic moments of their video.

As the nighttime crew change loomed, I grew apprehensive about what might happen. Would Bev show up on time? Would there be fireworks? Would they have made up? Could everybody swallow their pride for this final push to the finish?

A furious Bev actually arrived an hour early, but it didn't prevent an argument.

During the crew change, just before 10 p.m., Bev and Bruce stood in a church parking lot in Linden, Tennessee, hurling insults at each other. The camera crew caught every cuss word on tape.

"You will not give me ultimatums!" Bev screamed at Bruce. "You will not take me out of this race!"

The other members of the two crews continued to shift places, in silence. Bruce tried to move the argument away from me, but Bev wouldn't budge.

"I can, and I will, replace you," Bruce declared.

Crew explosions aren't uncommon in RAAM. One rider's mechanic quit early in the race in a dispute. Another crew person, weary of their cyclist's outbursts, simply quit on him in midrace. A crew member for another rider, commenting on my cheery demeanor, had offered to support me on my next RAAM adventure.

That mattered little as I stood there in the church parking lot, wishing that Mike and Rena would climb into a van and follow while I pedaled away. I was stunned. I'd had an uplifting moment with Bev, and now this? It wasn't the RAAM I envisioned. The squabbling would nag me the rest of the way, and I've never gotten over it.

I got back on my bike and waited to see who would follow me for the rest of the night. It was the night crew. They kept me going by offering bribes. Food had become a treat again, but by now the repetition had become dull.

But somewhere along the way they had raided a bakery of a few dozen sweet rolls. They were unbelievably tasty. My crew began to dangle the sweet rolls as incentive, saying they'd give me one if I made a certain checkpoint within a certain time frame.

Through it all, I kept thinking about Kish. I drove my crew crazy by repeatedly asking for his whereabouts. When the ninth morning of RAAM arrived, my crew gave me discouraging and encouraging news at the same time.

They informed me that Reed Finfrock, my riding buddy since Arizona and a competitor I hadn't seen since he sped past me in Arkansas with a team, had dropped out with 500 miles to go. I was at first relieved to know that I had one less competitor to worry about, but I was sad as well. I wanted to finish ahead of him, but I wanted him to finish. I thought about how strong he looked the previous day when I last saw him and wondered what the fates had in store for me.

Moments later I learned that Kish had finished at 8:19 a.m. We checked the maps. I had 513 miles to go. We did the quick math.

> *... yes! ... it's gonna be tough, but I can make it ... it's at my limit, but I can do it ... if I keep moving ...*

My spirits rose. I knew I could cover 513 miles in 48 hours, even though I was fading physically.

August 5-7, 1995
Chattanooga, Tennessee

Rob Kish arrives at the finish line in Savannah in eight days, 19 hours and 59 minutes—his slowest RAAM victory, thanks to oppressive heat at the beginning and Hurricane Erin before the finish ... The Kern Wheelmen, who started two days after the soloists, finish nearly three hours before him with a time of five days, 17 hours and five minutes ... Seana Hogan wins her fourth women's RAAM (9:04:17), nearly nine hours behind Kish and fourth overall ... Danny Chew and Gerry Tatrai are neck and neck approaching Savannah, with Chew (9:02:40) eventually prevailing by 36 minutes ... Muffy Ritz (9:06:32) is fifth overall, three hours behind Tatrai ... Dieter Weik is sixth (9:19:06), Tom Davies seventh (10:06:14), Bruno Heer eighth (10:11:37) with Beat Gfeller and George Thomas staging a sprint to the finish ... Kaname Sakurai and Rickey Wray Wilson also are still on the course, hoping to finish within the 48-hour window ... Ten soloists have dropped out due to dehydration and other medical ailments.

Chapter Nine

August 5-7, 1995

I was envious of Kish and the others who had finished as I pedaled in hot, humid and gloomy
weather from U.S. Highway 64 to Highway 41
toward Monteagle, about 40 miles west of Chattanooga. I
could picture Kish stretched out on a motel bed in Savannah, sleeping or eating a leisurely meal while I forged ahead.

I was also bored and imagined the crew to be just as
unexcited. The terrain had grown monotonous. My crews
were estranged. And we still had some 400 miles to go.

The sense of despair changed almost instantly when I
saw the sign: "Monteagle 4." Yes! I had ridden through
Monteagle on PAC Tour the previous summer, and I remembered how strong I felt on the steep four-mile climb
with hairpins toward the summit and then on the descent
into Tracy City. I knew at the top I would see Chattanooga, which in turn meant I was close to crossing into
Georgia, the final state. I stood up for the climb, peering
over the top of fogged glasses, summited, then descended
toward my parents' parked motor home at a convenience

George and his crew stop at a store in Tracy City to rest and restock.

store in Tracy City. I was ready for my final afternoon sleep break before for RAAM's final push.

When I awoke, I felt recharged. I knew this section of road from Team RAAM and PAC Tour. The weather was clear and mild. My crew told me I was catching Dieter Weik and had a chance for Rookie of the Year. They didn't even need to point me in the right direction, but as I approached the state line Mike leaped out of the van and out-sprinted me on foot to the first of several state crossings on the swiveling highway straddling the border. I had just enough of my faculties remaining to notice the blue sign with the big peach in the middle: Welcome to Georgia.

"Yo, Georgie," he said, "I know you feel like you're done, but you've still got 375 miles to go. That's a long time."

A long time indeed.

... Georgia! ... yes! ... finish feels so close,
yet so far ... Chattanooga was great ... love
seeing the big Georgia peach at the border ...
it's totally familiar now ... good news and bad
news ... good because I've been here before ...
bad because there's still a long way to go ...

After savoring a take-out meal from the Cracker Barrel Restaurant in Chattanooga, courtesy of my night crew, I pedaled south toward Atlanta on U.S. Highway 41, passing through Calhoun, Georgia. I'd been thinking about this point ever since West Memphis, when I was told that Kish had arrived at this northern Georgia time station.

As darkness descended, sleepiness began to take hold again. Deep in the Georgia woods, I saw a giant hand rise from under a bridge I was approaching. Behind the hand was a 60-foot-tall giant holding a pizza and smiling at me. I waved my crew forward and told them what I saw. They laughed, pointed at the stop sign that resembled a pizza and said, "Ride your bike."

Later that night, I saw a race official, dressed in white and softly glowing like a blowing sheet, by the side of the road, summoning me. I found the sight curious, because there was no wind. He yelled at me to come over, and I wondered why my crew was going past this time station. The race official then waved at me frantically, telling me he had some good dirt on my crew. I pulled an abrupt U-turn to the left, but as soon as I turned my handlebars, he was gone. I lost control of my bike and crashed into the passing lane on my left. I lay there, too exhausted to move, as Bev, Sabra and Eric raced to pull me away from the onrushing headlights.

The hallucinations had provided a good chuckle up to then. Now my crew feared for my safety.

I was deteriorating so badly again that I began to think 250 miles a day wouldn't be as easy as I anticipated. Could I still blow it at the end? This was my worst nightmare: I was so close, yet falling apart. Soon after, the night crew pulled into a used-car lot, suddenly thinking they were lost. They wanted to drive ahead and check the course. They left me in the parking lot with bag of popcorn, and when they returned they found me dozing in the driveway with my bicycle sprawled next to me.

Even as the sun rose on what promised to be my last day of RAAM, and I passed the outskirts of Atlanta, I was woozy and began drifting off to sleep on short descents. To stay awake I'd ask my crew for the progress of riders ahead of me.

At Covington, I took what I hoped would be my final nap. It was noon. Still 200 miles remained. I had 20 hours left in my window. I shifted into race mode.

... I can still make it ...

———————

On May 1, 1995, less than three months before RAAM was to begin, I was staying with my brother Sterling in The Dalles, Oregon, fearing the dream I so fervently pursued.

I told myself I should be excited. I had just received word that GlaxoSmithKline, maker of Lamictal, had agreed to sponsor my race. Serotta had committed to providing two bicycles and uniforms. Briko donated eyewear and helmets and Peak Sports in Corvallis was also on board. I had rounded up a crew. I was receiving tremendous support from a wide variety of generous people.

Trouble was, I hadn't trained nearly enough.

I was in decent shape from working as a ski instructor, but it was nowhere near what I needed to ride 2,911 miles. I also had put in some time on my indoor trainer and gotten out for two or three challenging rides, mostly 30 to 50 miles of climbing, but my total training miles numbered 2,000—less than one RAAM. My work schedule kept me too busy to train properly.

To get in some semblance of RAAM shape, I signed up for John Hughes's Pacific Crest Tour, a 13-day, 1,500-mile ride crisscrossing the Sierras from the Mexican border to Ashland, Oregon, in early June. I left my summer job as a ski instructor—Mount Hood has year-round skiing—and headed to Mexico.

I saw it as my only hope for successfully navigating the most arduous sporting event in the world.

If you had never heard of RAAM until now, you're not alone. Unlike the Tour de France stage race, the media have largely ignored it, except for in its infancy, when ABC filmed it for *Wide World of Sports*. Jim Lampley and Diana Nyad covered that first event, called "The Great American Bike Race."

RAAM's debut in 1982 was the consummated dream of four ultra-marathon cyclists who spent the previous several years trying to outdo each other riding coast to coast.

Its birth is traced to 1978, when southern California native John Marino, a onetime Los Angeles Dodgers prospect, set a transcontinental crossing record by pedaling from Santa Monica, California, to New York in 12 days and three hours. Marino made it in 1978 and 1980 and formed the Ultra-Marathon Cycling Association in the process. Marino then challenged John Howard, a three-time Olympic road cyclist and an Ironman champion, to a duel. The group grew to four with the addition of Michael Shermer, an adjunct professor from southern California's Occidental College whose claim to fame was setting a record for riding from Seattle to San Diego, and Lon Haldeman, an Illinois native and lifelong cycling fanatic whose cycling feat in 1981 would set the tone for RAAM.

Haldeman, now RAAM's race director, once owned 38 time trial records and rode 454 miles in a day on a banked oval track called a velodrome, but it was his road riding that amazed even the most ardent ultra-marathoners. In the summer of 1981, Haldeman announced that he planned to break Marino's Santa Monica-to-New York record. His warmup? Riding the same route from New York to Santa Monica.

Haldeman completed the first leg of his journey in 12 days, 18 hours and 47 minutes—easily breaking the unofficial east-to-west record of 15 days but falling shy of Marino's mark by about 15 hours. Undaunted, Haldeman grabbed a pizza and a nap at the Beverly Hills Hotel, hopped on his bicycle and headed east. He reached New York in a mind-boggling 10 days, 23 hours and 27 minutes, shattering a mark previously thought untouchable by nearly two days!

That achievement propelled the foursome into the first race on August 4, 1982. They were the only four entrants. Haldeman won in nine days, 20 hours and two minutes, some 15 hours ahead of Howard, 24 in front of Shermer and 59 in front of Marino. ABC captured every ache and pain from the first pedal stroke to the last, earning an Emmy Award for best sports documentary drama. Afterward, a teary-eyed Lampley called it the most emotionally moving event he had ever covered, and for the next four years ABC staffers fell all over themselves to get the assignment.

ABC received positive response from its coverage, but in 1986 the network declined to exercise the option on its contract, citing financial reasons. The timing was awful: The race had just secured a major sponsorship from

McDonald's, but the hamburger giant's stipulation was that RAAM have major television network coverage. In those days, before cable TV's explosion, that meant either ABC, NBC or CBS. None were interested. McDonald's backed out of its commitment, and the race has since been banished to the darkest recesses of America's sports consciousness.

I first read about RAAM in its inaugural year and always wondered if I could do it.

Early in the Pacific Crest Tour, I wilted in the heat that reached well past 100 in southern California, but eventually I began to ride into shape. When the PCT ended, I had never felt stronger.

I returned to my job on Mount Hood, ready and eager for RAAM—until one of my fellow skiing coaches showed me a color chart of the weather forecast for the race. The entire route was bathed in red, meaning temperatures over 100, and parts were maroon, for mercury above 110. People and cattle were dying across the South. I made a mental note to make sure we'd have enough ice.

I'd still only put in 3,500 miles of training by the time we packed the vans at Peak Sports in Corvallis and headed for Interstate 5 loaded with every conceivable piece of gear, including a purple mascot turtle named "George" and the rubber band I'd wear on my wrist to snap whenever I felt a hallucination coming on.

I didn't see the point of any more training. I didn't want to risk injury by over-training. Besides, I was confident I could finish my first solo RAAM.

After Covington, the miles just seemed to melt away. Two hundred. Then 150. Mike was updating me at each checkpoint. Relief washed over me as I realized that, barring a serious accident, I would finish within the 48-hour window, and each time I thought about it I rode a little faster.

The Georgia afternoon was perfect. No wind, a comfortable temperature, surprisingly low humidity and mostly flat terrain.

At mile 120, a cyclist joined me and we chatted briefly before he sprinted ahead. I chased him down, and he sprinted ahead again. I was irritated until I realized it was the race official manning the next time station. I was coming in ahead of schedule, catching him off guard. I'd be the 10th and final official solo finisher out of 19 men and three women who started the race, but no matter. I felt great.

With 100 miles to go, a reporter and photographer from the Dublin, Ga., *Courier-Herald* began to leapfrog me, and a nice afternoon turned into a glorious evening. I was so relaxed that I took an extended bathroom break, only to be exhorted on by my anxious crew.

I soon realized I was rapidly gaining on the rider ahead of me. I thought it was Dieter Weik, but it turned out to be Beat Gfeller of Switzerland. Everybody's mood was set on high.

Ironically, 2,800 miles into the toughest sporting event in the world, I was having one of the best rides of my life.

> *... cadence is steady ... I'm actually going to finish ... I actually feel like a RAAM rider ... can't think of anything I'd rather be doing ... it's gorgeous ... Savannah isn't far now ...*

The euphoria lasted to the time station in Metter, Georgia, where my neck began to hurt for the first time since Oklahoma. I noticed my swollen feet for the first time and could feel my toenails loose in my shoes. I asked Rena for a quick rubdown and was chided by a guy in the camera crew.

*At the finish line in Savannah, George and his crew celebrate
his completion of the 1995 solo RAAM.*

"You've only got 50 miles to go!"

> *... yeah, well, you ride 50 miles ... I need*
> *a break and I've still got three hours of riding*
> *left ... I don't want to ride another three hours*
> *... I want to be done ...*

When I got back on my bike, Bruce told me that Gfeller, who led me by 14 hours in western Oklahoma, was only 18 miles ahead. I heard eight. I thought I could catch him quickly. Even though my body was completely fried, I decided to pursue him, attempting to ride the final 52 miles at 20 to 25 mph in an attempt to catch him. It wasn't until later that I learned that Bruce hadn't been entirely honest with me and that the gap had actually been 28 miles.

"I didn't want him to think Gfeller was out of range, so I lied about the mileage to keep George motivated," Bruce told the film crew. "It was the only time during the race that I lied to him."

My heart quickened when my father called from the Road Trek's cell phone to say he had spotted Gfeller.

"He can barely keep his bike on the road! He's barely moving," he said excitedly, then added moments later: "He's down! Tell George, Gfeller's off his bike!" Already struggling, Gfeller was forced by race officials to sit idly for 15 minutes because of an earlier infraction. When his time expired, he was so weak he had to be helped into his saddle.

His speed had dropped to five mph. Transformed by the news, I gained quickly. As I passed the final time station, 11 miles outside of Savannah, I was told I was closing in on Gfeller. I searched the horizon for the lights of his van in the darkness.

My feelings about catching Gfeller were mixed. My competitive side loved the hunt. Yet I couldn't imagine how disappointed he'd be to get caught in Savannah. I silently hoped I wouldn't catch him, yet still tried with my last vestiges of energy. The point was moot. Somehow, Gfeller coaxed a final burst from his depleted mind, body and spirit. I never saw him.

Savannah.

I knew the road well, and felt I could navigate it blind-folded. The night was warm and completely calm. I rode over the bridge on the outskirts of town and into the city, which was devoid of traffic after 1 a.m.

> *… savor this … you'll never know a feeling like this again in your life … can't wait to finish, but I wish this feeling could last forever … don't crash on the cobblestones! …*

A van arrived from the opposite direction carrying Mike and Cindy Rourke, race officials who asked to escort me to the finish line in front of the Hyatt Regency Hotel. I made the final turn and noticed a small crowd at the finish line, thanks partly to Gfeller finishing 15 minutes ahead of me. Bittersweet feelings engulfed me as I finally rolled across the finish line in 10th place overall and eighth among solo men, 10 days, 13 hours and 43 minutes after starting in Irvine—six hours within the 48-hour window.

It was 1:43 a.m.

About 25 or 30 people were there, including Reed Finfrock, who drove to the finish and waited up to greet me. Gfeller's Swiss crew gave me a rousing cheer.

But there was no Bev. I scanned the area around the courthouse in Savannah, but I couldn't find her. The split with the crew had exacted a toll, and she was in a motel room. She asked to be called before I was arrived, but no one bothered until after I crossed the finish line. Here was my biggest moment in sports, and the most important person in my life wasn't there until well after I crossed the finish line. I was wracked with a wide variety of emotions, and I was in intense physical pain, but I didn't want the camera crew to see it. This was an intensely personal and private time.

After pictures and congratulations, I lay down on the brick hotel steps overlooking the Savannah River and fell asleep in my filthy cycling clothes.

After photos and congratulations, exhaustion takes over and George sleeps on the steps of the hotel overlooking the Savannah River.

C h a p t e r   T e n

RAAM Epilogue

When I finally awoke on the steps of the Savannah Hyatt in the wee hours, I found myself consumed by a strange and surprising sense of profound sadness.

RAAM was over. Instead of relief, my world had a gaping void. I'd wanted to ride solo in the Race Across America since I first read about it 13 years earlier. Now that I'd accomplished a feat that had dominated my dreams for years and every last ounce of my fiber for the previous 10 days, I was left with a hollow feeling. What would I do with myself now?

It was an emptiness I hadn't experienced the two previous years after my RAAM relays. Nor would I have it after finishing the race on a tandem bicycle in 2000 and 2002. I'll probably never know it again.

All I could think about was how much I wanted to do RAAM again. Never mind that my neck ached, my knees were swollen and my feet hurt. I began to think about the 1996 RAAM. I contemplated how I might finish in less than 10 days. I was suddenly struck by how much my time mattered to me. When I was younger, I'd make a note of my marks in cross-country or bicycle races, but never did they motivate me to train harder. Now, after 3,000 miles of pedaling, I just wanted to get back on my bicycle.

The morning after RAAM ended, my crew dispersed in different directions and returned to their lives. I went back to Corvallis, where I took a job in the bicycle shop at Peak Sports, thinking that as the days passed I would eventually shake the pit in my stomach. I didn't, and Bev was nonplussed. She hoped RAAM was out of my system and we could get on with our lives. I had her and a four-year-old daughter to support. If I'd start to talk about the 1996 RAAM, Bev would chastise me for my selfishness. It was time, she insisted, to move on.

Certainly I could understand. RAAM wasn't likely to put food on our table or clothe Meredith. RAAM's place in the American sporting consciousness was negligible. Few people have ever heard of it, even among sports fanatics. Rob Kish is not an American superstar. People who do know something about the event are sure we're missing a few links in our chains. RAAM cyclists compete for the personal glory and fulfillment, not for the hype, money or endorsements. Our local newspaper, the *Corvallis Gazette-Times*, did a few stories that I've got in my scrapbook, and it was fun to talk about RAAM upon my return with the few people who asked, but there was no hero's welcome.

That was okay with me. That wasn't why I did RAAM either.

The hollowness lasted through the summer and autumn, then carried into the winter. Working in the bike shop at Peak Sports was fun because I was around bicycle people, but it was also frustrating because I couldn't join them on rides through the lush coastal foothills of the Willamette Valley on our beautiful fall days. RAAM exacts a heavy price for those 10 days, but the toll doesn't end at the finish line. My knees and feet were swollen for weeks. Riding a bicycle was painful because of my bruised crotch. I couldn't hold my head up for weeks. It took longer to get any dexterity back in my hands because of nerve damage. They still tremble slightly to this day.

The emotional fallout is just as intense. It was at least a month before my sleep patterns returned to normal. I'd wake up abruptly in the middle of the night, thinking I'd overslept, that I'd lost time and needed to get back on the bike. My sound sleep was permeated by strange dreams. One night I dreamt my crew was taking a sleep break along a river and my bicycle was floating away on a raft. I woke up in a panic.

I was getting antsy. RAAM continued to dominate my thoughts and haunt my dreams. I was left with the feeling that there was more to accomplish, even though I had at long last completed my personal journey, 11 years after it began on that San Antonio street in front of Tracy Williams's house.

Because I had competed in RAAM, my emotional pendulum had swung 180 degrees from the depths of my physical and emotional rehabilitation from the car wreck in 1984 and the seizures in 1989. By finishing, I had found my equilibrium. I had set and met a difficult goal, one I would never forget. I had overcome intense pain, brutal weather, sleep deprivation and RAAM's intangible demons. Winner Rob Kish, who had competed in 10 RAAMs, called it his most challenging because of the conditions. I was impressed with myself for finishing the world's toughest event under its most dismal conditions. Indeed, I was grateful the race had been so grueling because, after all, that's why I was there.

Different sensations had kept me going: Fear of quitting, proving to myself and others that I could do it, not wanting to let down my crew and sponsors. But the biggest factor was the intestinal fortitude I never had before the car accident in 1984. When every reasoned voice is telling you to quit and you can still keep going, it's an emotional peak that's difficult to hit in everyday life. If RAAM had been easy, it wouldn't have been an accomplishment. If everybody could do it, it wouldn't be special.

I had nothing left to prove to myself, and indeed, while I was proud of my RAAM ring I saw no reason to wear it. It really did seem like an appropriate time to put RAAM on its proper pedestal and move on.

Yet I simply couldn't. There were several reasons why. I always loved sports, and this was a sport I did well—a race not many people can do, much less finish. I also didn't know what else to do with my life. I had a college degree but little interest in pursuing my major as a career. There was that nagging void, the mystical magnetism of RAAM. For some, once it's in your blood it's difficult to exorcise.

And then there was Jim Bunn.

Bunn was a Georgia resident who joined my RAAM team in 1995 as the director of the GlaxoSmithKline camera crew.

Now a correspondent for MSNBC, Bunn began the race skeptical of my undertaking. Like most people, the camera crew had no clue what it was about. It was a job. Over time, they became engrossed in the event. Bunn was so captivated that he began to write about the race as we moved into the Plains. They went beyond the filming of RAAM to becoming a part of it. Ultimately, they became a part of our team. On the last night, they were more involved than ever, filming every dramatic moment. They weren't about to miss the finish.

Afterward, Bunn began telling me that I could have a career as a public speaker. As he and his partners shot video of RAAM, he told me he liked the way I came across on camera. He said he had intended to hire a professional talent for a voice-over but decided instead to stick with raw footage of me. He told me that after the video was finally released, I could write a book and give talks to epilepsy patients, pharmaceutical companies and epilepsy foundations, among other groups. They would find my story inspiring. Eventually he would find me an agent. Just keep training and working at the bike shop, he implored.

Jim Bunn was providing my uncertain future with an unexpected energy and excitement that kept me tuned into RAAM. He was the reason I stayed at Peak Sports. Be patient, he kept saying. When Bev and I would get anxious about finances, he would convince me that better days were ahead. He wanted me to keep racing.

It felt strange to have a video made about me, particularly when I knew I would look so trashed through most of it. I felt self-conscious about the attention. But Bunn's work was impressive. The video was gripping. People who saw it were mesmerized by my cross-country adventure. I began to believe a career as an ultra-marathon bicyclist and public speaker was possible, and the more I considered the idea the more I liked it. Even Bev was enthused.

Bunn also convinced me that my visibility and story could do more than make a living for me. He said I could help people with epilepsy as well as the people who are charged with treating it. There are numerous inspirational books and movies out there about people who have overcome challenges—most notably Lance Armstrong's incredible recovery from cancer to win four consecutive Tour de France crowns—but for the stigmatized disorder called epilepsy there was a huge void.

I could have a future in racing and speaking, filling one void by filling another in the world of epilepsy.

After the 1995 RAAM, GlaxoSmithKline organized a media tour for me. The company's public relations department set up conference calls or television interviews. I was repeatedly asked about the seemingly paradoxical concept of a person with epilepsy racing a bicycle across America. I was also hired to give an occasional talk, including one in my hometown of San Antonio. The early audiences consisted mostly of people in the medical community, epilepsy patients and their families. It was exciting, fun and comfortable, and the reaction was overwhelmingly enthusiastic.

One couple approached me with tears in their eyes. They told me they finally understood what their two-year-old daughter was experiencing with epilepsy. Another woman told me she didn't have epilepsy, but that my presentation motivated her to lose weight. In San Francisco, a group leader asked the audience to share what risks they, like me, had taken in spite of their fears.

Jim Bunn was right. I began to think I truly was doing something worthwhile.

Bunn felt continuing to race was important for my speaking career because my 1995 RAAM achievement would eventually fade. It's exactly what I wanted to hear. I loved the challenges and the freedom of the open road. The only resistance was at home, where Bev was still worried about money and wasn't keen on a life with a bicycle nomad. My concession was to shelve the idea of riding in the 1996 RAAM. I was still so beat up from 1995 that I wasn't sure I could properly prepare anyway.

In April 1996, eight months after my solo finish in RAAM, I entered the Hope Race, a 535-miler from Boston to Washington D.C. Because I was still feeling the effects of RAAM, I had less than 200 miles of training.

Nevertheless, I flew to Boston and met with a makeshift crew of volunteers from Boston. I rode well for about 200 miles, nearly "bonked," and then put all of my RAAM experiences to use to finish the race. I kept telling myself I'd ridden farther in 1995, so I certainly could cover 535 miles. It was definitely a change in the way I thought about ultra-marathons. I reminded myself that I only had to ride for a day. I knew I had reserves to finish. RAAM had shown me that. I finished fourth and realized how tough I could be.

Two months later, Bev and I were in the process of buying a house in Corvallis and I was still training only 80 miles a week, much of it towing Meredith in our Burley trailer. I still had one foot in racing and one out. Time wouldn't allow me to fully commit. I had a job, a family and this vague concept of a career in racing and public speaking. I still felt in limbo.

Late in the spring of 1996, one of my sponsors, Serotta, suggested I compete that June in the Midnight Sun 600K from Anchorage to Fairbanks, Alaska. I hesitated. I was eager to see Alaska, but I was in so-so condition. I pondered it for days before relenting. Much to my surprise, I played leapfrog with the machine-like Wolfgang Fasching for nearly 250 miles. I rolled into Fairbanks in second place in 20 hours and 19 minutes, about an hour behind Fasching, the Lance Armstrong of ultra-marathon bicycle racing. I stayed with him for a long time. I had refused to let him ride away. RAAM had changed my competitive mindset.

I finished second, third and fourth in ultra-marathon races that year. I entered the 24 Hours of Adrenaline mountain bike race and placed third even though I had only trained for two weeks on a "fat-tire" bike. But I had done RAAM. I knew in my heart that I could ride for 24 hours.

RAAM gave me a confidence I never had in athletics. I had evolved from thinking "I can't win" to thinking "I can."

Cycling observers marveled that I could perform so well with epilepsy. I quietly agreed. I was enjoying the accolades and was satisfied with the results.

After I returned from Alaska, I received a phone call from my longtime friend John Hughes. I expected Hughes, one of the top names in endurance racing, to pat me on the back for finishing second in Alaska despite meager training. I anticipated he would be impressed that a guy with epilepsy could fend off so many "normal" riders.

I was wrong.

Hughes chastised me for using epilepsy as a crutch, as an excuse to avoid training the way I should. It had actually been pretty arrogant, and perhaps even stupid, to enter RAAM in 1995 with only six weeks of training. Hughes said I was settling for being "a good rider with epilepsy." He wanted me to stop thinking of myself as great for a guy with epilepsy and start thinking of myself as a great rider.

The criticism caught me off guard, but I realized he was right. I was settling for being a good rider with epilepsy. I could do more.

Epilepsy no longer was my excuse to settle for merely finishing. It had been okay for people to say, "Wow, I can't believe you're out there with epilepsy!" It was even better for people to say, "Wow, you have epilepsy and you won." Thanks to John Hughes I realized my personal mission wasn't fulfilled. I wanted to be known, and know myself as, an outstanding cyclist. Period. Epilepsy would merely be the sidebar to a racing story.

I continued to take medication, of course, but epilepsy ceased to play a role in my races. Longtime crew members and supporters never talked about it, except to occasionally remind me to take my Lamictal. Before one race, Mike Kloeppel's sister Gretchen, who had just joined my crew as massage therapist, cocked an eyebrow when she heard Mike wondering aloud if I'd taken my medication.

"Medication?" she said anxiously. "For what?"

"George has epilepsy," Mike replied.

"What if he has a seizure?" Gretchen asked, surprised and concerned.

Mike shrugged. He was more concerned with the real threats to my racing: My nutrition, my neck and my Achilles tendon. That's what I worry about, too. Epilepsy had virtually dropped off our radar screens on the road, consciously and subconsciously. I thought about it only when I had to take my medication.

The successes in Alaska and elsewhere were fulfilling, but ultimately they only contributed to the void that persisted since I rose from the steps of the Savannah Hyatt on that balmy night in August 1995. More than ever, I thought about facing the challenges and demons of RAAM. I wondered how I'd fare with serious training behind me.

The topic was taboo at home, but I had a yearning that would only be satiated by RAAM. I couldn't explain it. Still can't. Only RAAM competitors understand it.

In the winter of 1996, Glaxo and another sponsor, Soft Ride, came to me with an idea: Ride in the 1997 RAAM.

I said yes.

Chapter Eleven

Moving Forward

My dream of competing in the 1997 Race Across America was shattered—literally—in February.

I was training in the foothills northwest of my home in Corvallis when I crashed at 40 mph on frozen fog on a descent. I could hear my collarbone grind on the pavement as I slid down Sulphur Springs Road. When my body finally came to a halt, I tried to move it myself but couldn't. Pain shot through my shoulder. My stomach was queasy. My helmet was in at least a dozen pieces.

When help finally arrived, I was driven to the emergency room at Good Samaritan Hospital in Corvallis, where the doctor and I began to have light banter after the drugs eased my pain. I was enjoying his company until he discovered I was on medication for epilepsy. He instantly went cold. He questioned whether I had really hit ice. He didn't believe me. He was convinced I had a seizure. Eight years after the last seizure, the stigma of epilepsy lingered.

In the coming weeks, I began to see a physical therapist to help mend my shoulder. At one point she asked what I did for a living. I told her that I raced bicycles and gave speeches. I described the car accident and the seizures. She told me I was fortunate that I only had seizures. At least, she said supportively, I didn't have epilepsy. I was dumbfounded by the lack of compassion. This was a person in the medical community.

Episodes like this are frequent for those of us with epilepsy, and they served to remind me about the importance of my message and to make sure I remained a visible, credible speaker with a story to tell. My 1995 RAAM drama would always be compelling, but I had to keep my resume current. I had to keep racing.

Even without such misunderstandings, epilepsy will never completely leave my psyche. It's always there. Not a day goes by when I don't think about it. Never is there a day when I don't wonder if, or when, I'll have another seizure. Even if I never have another seizure, there's always a reminder in my medicine cabinet. I'll take three pills every day for the rest of my life. That's down from a combination of 16 during my investigational trial in 1989, but still a ubiquitous reminder.

Occasionally someone will ask me when I'll no longer need medication. It's not an option. I have no reason to stop. My health isn't broken, so I see no reason to fix it.

I don't dwell on having epilepsy, but I can still feel the violent dizzy spells and seizures as if they happened yesterday. I can still sense the humility of relinquishing my driver's license. I can still see the looks in people's eyes when they've learned I have epilepsy. I still wear the stigma with people who don't understand.

Once, on a flight from Oregon to North Carolina, I had an odd dream and woke up in a cold sweat with an upset stomach. Most people might assume they had air-sickness. Everybody has senses of déjà vu, but when my stomach gets queasy or I have a dizzy spell, I think, "Uh, oh, is it coming back?"

It's frightening sometimes, but I'm among the lucky ones. I don't have seizures any more. I speak to people who have them every month, every week, every day.

I try to use RAAM and my other experiences to motivate my audiences, but not to inspire them to be like me. Hope comes in myriad forms. For one person it might mean reducing the number of seizures per month. For another it's eliminating side affects. For yet another perhaps it's learning about all the treatment options available. For still others it's about understanding how to improve communication with their doctors.

I encourage people to find their physical and emotional equilibrium, whether it's pedaling a bicycle across the country, taking a walk around the block or finding another slice of enjoyment where it might have been lacking.

Mostly, my message is about improving quality of life. There are 2.1 million of us, and far too many see ourselves as victims or are treated as such. I talk about possibilities and solutions and hope.

Racing a bicycle extraordinary distances, and doing it well, has become my vehicle to share a message of hope for people with epilepsy. Drawing from the lessons of my own life and the daunting challenges of my Race Across America in 1995, I encourage audiences to approach their lives one breath, one pedal stroke, one hour at a time.

*With Mt. McKinley in the background, George pedaled to a first-place
finish in the Midnight Sun 600K from Anchorage to Fairbanks in 1997.*

*George and his BAM crew, Darren Snyder (left) and
Mike Kloeppel (right) after the race in 1997.*

Following my own advice, I continued to train with
more fervor than ever. I pedaled in miserable weather
around the Willamette Valley wearing a sling on my in-
jured shoulder.

In June, I returned to my signature race, Alaska's Midnight Sun 600K, not with the intention of performing
well as a cyclist with epilepsy, but with the intention of
winning. I was eager to see if my training would pay divi-
dends. Never had I entered a race with so much convic-
tion. Simply riding a hard 375 miles was no longer a satis-
fying accomplishment. I had a singular goal. I openly
hoped that Wolfgang Fasching would return.

The 1997 Midnight Sun 600K was another turning point in my life. I was fit, I had no hallucinations and I raced for the entire distance. Unlike in 1996, when I marveled at the scenery, the views of Mount McKinley and the wildlife, I focused entirely on the road. I won going away. My time was 19 hours, 15 minutes and 58 seconds. I was off the bike only six minutes.

Not even the absence of Fasching could dampen my spirit.

Later that summer I entered the rugged Bicycle Across Missouri, a deceptively challenging 575-mile race from Saint Louis to Kansas City and back again. The race featured short steep climbs and hot sticky weather. Despite taking numerous wrong turns I won BAM in 33 hours and 58 minutes.

Unfortunately, the Midnight Sun 600K met its demise after the 1997 event when the man who created and organized the race as a labor of love decided he'd had enough. I mourned briefly and then decided to use the open June racing window as an opportunity. In 1998, I created the bicycle Race Across Oregon, a benefit for The Epilepsy Foundation of Oregon. It began as a competitive training ride for me against a relay team of four top cyclists from Corvallis, but the resulting media coverage and response from the public was significant enough to consider turning RAO into an annual event.

I lost that 435-mile race, but the Race Across Oregon won. It has become one of two RAAM qualifiers in the West, along with Furnace Creek. Cyclists from as far away as Italy have traveled to Oregon to compete on what I'm told is the most challenging ultra-distance course in the nation.

As my racing stock rose, I became intrigued about upping the ante in RAAM. If there is anything more challenging than competing solo, it's riding on a tandem bi-

George rolls to an easy win in the 1997 Bike Across Missouri.

In preparation for the 2000 RAAM, George and his tandem partner,
Katie Lindquist, raced at the 24-Hour World Championships in Iowa.

cycle. Tandem riders not only must pedal in sync for 3,000 miles in RAAM, but must be together mentally as well. It's ideal when both riders are on a high, okay when one carries the other, but debilitating if both are suffering. You're completely reliant on your partner. What an irony. A onetime loner liked the idea of working together toward an accomplishment. RAAM had brought me out of that shell, too.

In 1999, I asked one of my new sponsors, Co-Motion Cycles of Eugene, Oregon, if they knew of any women who might be interested in the RAAM. I had tried riding tandem with male riders and couldn't find the right chemistry. I was looking for a partner with the same mental approach I had and someone I could get along with for two weeks on a bicycle.

Co-Motion directed me to a powerful mountain bike racer from Plymouth, Minnesota, named Katie Lindquist, who was training in the high altitude of Steamboat Springs, Colorado. We talked on the phone, hit it off immediately and decided to go for it. We met for the first time in September 1999 at the 24-Hour World Championships in Iowa. We then went out and set a record. We weren't necessarily ready for RAAM, but we decided to do it anyway.

Five years after my solo RAAM venture, I returned to the event with Katie. We completed the race, this time from Portland, Oregon, to Pensacola, Florida, in 11 days and 16 hours. The time was a full day slower than my solo crossing, but the course was much more challenging be-

George experiences "Shermer Neck" through Colorado during the 2000 RAAM.

cause of the climbs in Oregon, Utah and Colorado. I was now the only rider in RAAM history to finish solo, on a relay team and on a tandem.

Unfortunately, Bev never could reconcile with my new lifestyle. We drifted apart emotionally. Not long after the 2000 RAAM, we separated. A few months later, at a cycling camp in Arizona, I met Terri Gooch, a New Yorker who shares my goals. Terri's determination and strength have helped me take my training and goals to yet another level. She also inspired me to compete in RAAM again. After taking 2001 off, we began preparations for 2002. In less than a year, we rode more than 15,000 miles.

My fifth RAAM was as close to perfect as possible. I say "close to perfect" because it had its own set of obstacles. Terri and I suffered relatively few physical problems. Those we had were prepared for and fixed quickly. Mentally, we were usually in sync and any disagreements we had were talked about until we solved them. Our relationship actually grew stronger as the race progressed and we faced the challenges of RAAM together. This wasn't always easy.

Our primary goal was the RAAM mixed-tandem record. We knew it would be difficult, as the mountainous 2,992-mile Portland to Pensacola course, which contains more than 100,000 feet of climbing, is not suited to tandem. After maintaining record pace through the first half of the course, we and our crew were confident that the record was in our grasp. This confidence began to fade as we left the halfway town of Walsenberg, Colorado, where we were caught by a freak windstorm. The round-the-clock 30-40 mph head- and crosswinds often slowed us to a crawl, and for three days our daily mileage was barely 200. RAAM 2002 ended up being one of the slowest in the 20-year history of the race. Pushing through the wind was physically and mentally exhausting. Our frequent conver-

Terri and George wearily embrace after completing the 2002 RAAM.

sations came to an end as it became impossible to hear each other over the noise of the wind. The tandem, where we have always felt so close, became very lonely. Once out of the wind, however, we reconnected. We finished strong, covering the final 336 miles in 22 hours. When our shot at the record was blown away, we rearranged our goals from being record setters to official finishers. After all the training we put in, it was difficult at first to find satisfaction in a finishing time three hours slower than my tandem time in 2000. With half the field having dropped out, we realized that we had finished an extremely difficult race. We won our division and became only the second tandem in nine years to finish RAAM.

I'm now convinced there's no such thing as the perfect RAAM. Life certainly is imperfect, and as a microcosm of life, so is the Race Across America. Perhaps that's why we thirst for more. We're always in search for the perfect race, just as life is the pursuit of perfection.

Truth is, though, no RAAM experience, regardless how close to perfection, could equal my sense of accomplishment in 1995. It will forever remain in its own emotional trophy case, untouchable.

In the years since I crossed the finish line, many of the tangible elements have faded. I've lost track of most of my crew, with the exception of my parents, who were faithful followers on all my races until the 2002 RAAM, when my mother's health forced them to remain in San Antonio. They've yet to see Terri and me race. My Aunt Georgiann is still a teacher in Nebraska. Sabra is now a veterinarian in Corvallis, and though we remain friends we don't see each other often. Rena Andrews is still a massage therapist in The Dalles, Oregon. Eric Larsen, our night mechanic, vanished in northern Minnesota after the race and I haven't heard from him since. I'm still close with Mike Kloeppel, who was in my crew for the Race Across

Oregon, The Midnight Sun 600K and Bike Across Missouri. But he's now working full-time for a bicycle accessories company in Tacoma, Washington, where he has a wife, a young child and no time to join me on my cycling adventures. Sadly, in the bitter wake of our crew dysfunction, crew chief Bruce Franklin, whom I once counted as one of my best friends, and I have lost touch. The last I heard he was working for an Oregon winery.

Such is RAAM. It brings complete strangers together, thrusts them into intimate proximity for two weeks, and then sends them off to their worlds. My story isn't unusual in that sense.

Will I ever do RAAM again? I don't know. For sure, I'll never do it solo. On a tandem, perhaps, if Terri is willing. My attitude toward RAAM has changed. It has become more of a business. My solo ride in 1995 was about physical, emotional and spiritual gain.

Why we do it remains an individual mystery. In 2002, outside of Kim, Oklahoma, where the crosswinds were blowing at 40 mph, pushing us into oncoming traffic and forcing us to walk our tandem bicycle, a weary Terri asked why we were there. I had no rational answer. "Because it's there," is a cliché, and it doesn't fit. Many things are "there" and I don't do them. I have no desire to climb Mount Everest. Honestly, I've never asked anyone else why they do it, and I've never been able to answer the question for myself.

The best analogy I can think of is the old myth about a king who wanted to be a god. Believing he was the strongest and wisest man in the world, he boldly proclaimed he could overcome whatever obstacles were placed in his path to become a god. His task: To stay awake for one week. He lasted one day. It takes more than sheer strength and wisdom to finish RAAM.

Whatever the reason for RAAM's magnetism, I know this: I rehash portions of my 1995 journey from California to Georgia every day. It towers above my other accomplishments, including my four other RAAM finishes.

After every other race, I was happy it was over. After the first relay in 1993, I was excited we won but felt unfulfilled. After the second relay in 1994, the team was so fractured I was just glad to be done. After my first tandem ride in 2000, I was disappointed that Katie Lindquist and I had quarreled as we neared the finish. And even after my tandem ride with Terri in 2002, captured forever in a snapshot that shows us tearfully embracing on the steps in Pensacola, I was happy to be done and eager to get on with our lives.

George and his crew celebrate at the Savannah finish line after he completed the 1995 solo RAAM.

RAAM '95 was different for what it represented then and represents now.

Today, I can elicit vivid images of the event with little effort. I can still feel the intense heat of the Mojave Desert, the burning of my skin and the queasiness in my stomach. I can smell the night air of northern Arizona and feel the throbbing in my Achilles. I can still feel the anguish toward my crew in the Four Corners area. I can sense the power of my climb up Wolf Creek Pass and the demoralizing descent on the other side.

I can envision the punishing rolling prairies of Oklahoma's panhandle, the gale-force winds in the deceptively gentle hills of Arkansas, the grandeur of the Mississippi River bridge, the camaraderie of riding with Reed and the excitement of crossing the Georgia state line—all as if it happened yesterday.

Most of all, I can picture myself pedaling toward Savannah in the wee hours of a balmy southern summer night. I can see the lights of the city in the distance. I can smell the humid air and feel the ambience of the historic town squares and cobblestones. I can feel the warm steps of the Savannah Hyatt.

I remember the mix of emotions, feeling so ecstatic over finishing and yet realizing I'll never, ever, know a moment like that again. I remember the sense of magic at the finish, the same feeling I had at the beginning in California. I remember wanting to freeze-frame the feelings of happiness and sadness, of contentment and fatigue, of relief and glory, forever.

For me, it was much, much more than just a Race Across America.

I still get butterflies in the pit of my stomach just thinking about it.

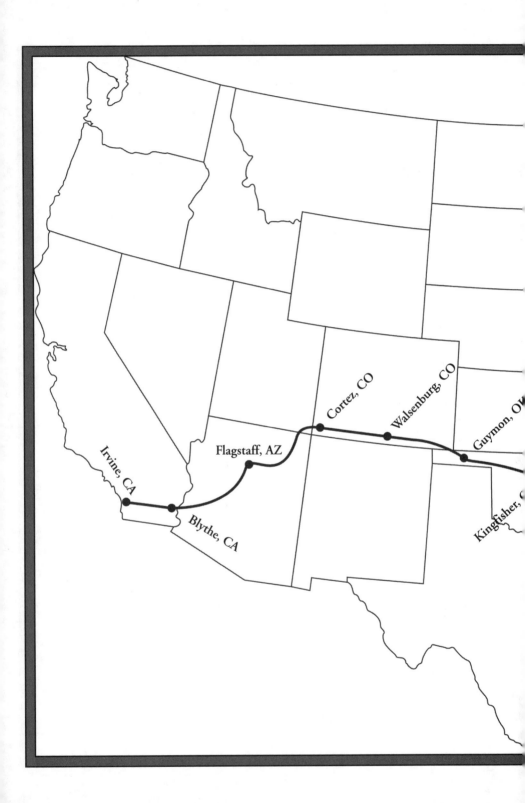

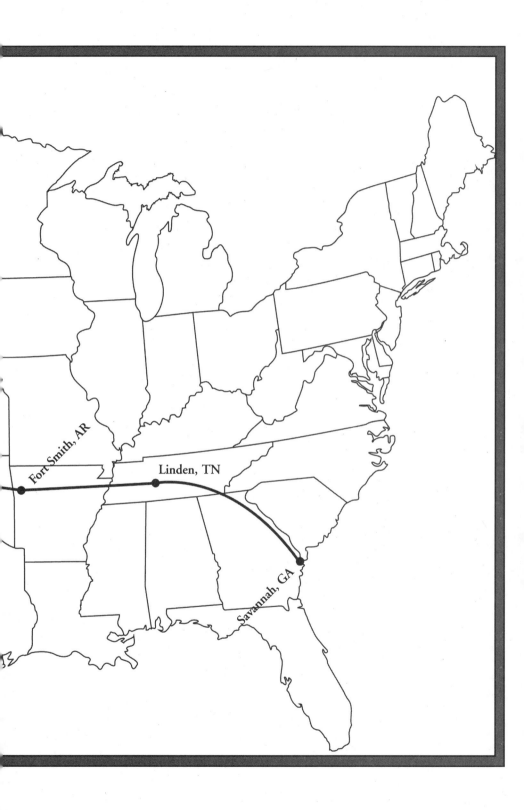

Celebrate the Heroes of Sports
in These Other Titles from Sports Publishing!

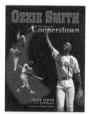

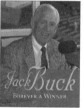
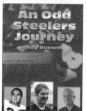

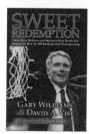